# OKLAHOMA STATE

# DAILY DEVOTIONS FOR DIE-HARD FANS

# COWBOYS

***Daily Devotions for Die-Hard Fans***
**Also Available:**

## ACC
*Clemson Tigers*
*Duke Blue Devils*
*FSU Seminoles*
*Georgia Tech Yellow Jackets*
*North Carolina Tar Heels*
*NC State Wolfpack*
*Virginia Cavaliers*
*Virginia Tech Hokies*

## BIG 10
*Michigan Wolverines*
*Ohio State Buckeyes*

## BIG 12
*Oklahoma Sooners*
*Oklahoma State Cowboys*
*TCU Horned Frogs*
*Texas Longhorns*
*Texas Tech Red Raiders*

## SEC
*Alabama Crimson Tide*
*Arkansas Razorbacks*
*Auburn Tigers*
*More Auburn Tigers*
*Florida Gators*
*Georgia Bulldogs*
*Kentucky Wildcats*
*LSU Tigers*
*More Georgia Bulldogs*
*Mississippi State Bulldogs*
*Ole Miss Rebels*
*South Carolina Gamecocks*
*More South Carolina Gamecocks*
*Texas A&M Aggies*
*Tennessee Volunteers*

OKLAHOMA STATE

*Daily Devotions for Die-Hard Fans: Oklahoma State Cowboys*
© 2013 Ed McMinn
Extra Point Publishers; P.O. Box 871; Perry GA 31069

Library of Congress Cataloging-in-Publication Data
13 ISBN Digit ISBN: 978-09882595-3-9

Unless otherwise noted, scripture quotations are taken from the
*Holy Bible, New International Version.* Copyright © 1973, 1978, 1984,
by the International Bible Society. All rights reserved.

Go to http://www.die-hardfans.com for information about other
titles in the series.

Cover design by John Powell.

Every effort has been made to identify copyright
holders. Any omissions are unintentional.
Extra Point Publishers should be notified in
writing immediately for full acknowledgement.

COWBOYS

# OKLAHOMA STATE

# DAILY DEVOTIONS FOR DIE-HARD FANS

# COWBOYS

# IN THE BEGINNING

**Read Genesis 1, 2:1-3.**

*"God saw all that he had made, and it was very good" (v. 1:31).*

In the beginning, the press praised Henry Iba as the savior of a downtrodden Oklahoma A&M basketball program. Little reason existed, however, for such optimism.

In the spring of 1934, a basketball referee submitted Iba's name as a candidate for the head coach's position in Stillwater. After a private interview, the school president offered Iba the job, and he took it. The Oklahoma press proclaimed Iba the "savior who could work miracles overnight." A reality check suggested, however, an outcome other than success, immediate or otherwise.

The basketball program's last winning season had been in 1928. The student newspaper scathingly referred to the team's "stranglehold on the cellar of the Missouri Valley Conference." In 1933-34, the team had finished last in the league with a 4-14 record.

Much of the problem lay in the facilities. The gym was not adequate for major sports competition. The court was small and seating was limited to about 2,000 comfortably. For games such as those against Oklahoma that drew an overflow crowd, adventuresome spectators "crawled out onto the metal girders which supported the roof, literally filling the hall to the rafters." Thus, the program consistently lost money.

Another problem for the new head coach lay in his players.

They weren't tall, and "no natural talents existed among the let-termen." He had some good athletes, but "offensive skills in basketball were notably lacking."

Thus, Iba didn't buy into the media's extravagant hopes, and he cautiously and realistically shied away from promising even a winning season in 1935. The team went 9-9, which was certainly a vast improvement. That was the beginning of the Iba era in Stillwater that lasted 36 seasons with 655 wins, fifteen conference titles, and national championships in 1945 and '46.

As Henry Iba's success demonstrated, beginnings are important. What we make of them, however, is even more important. Consider, for example, how far the State basketball program has come since that first practice session in 1935.

Every morning, without even thinking about it, you get a gift from God: a new beginning. God hands to you as an expression of divine love a new day full of promise and the chance to right the wrongs in your life. You can use the day to pay a debt, start a new relationship, replace a burned-out light bulb, tell your family you love them, chase a dream, solve a nagging problem . . . or not.

God simply provides the gift. How you use it is up to you. People often talk wistfully about starting over or making a new beginning. God gives you the chance with the dawning of every new day. You have the chance today to make things right – and that includes your relationship with God.

*His 'glum forecasts' prophesied no better than a .500 season ahead.*
*-- On Henry Iba's expectations for his first season in Stillwater*

**Every day is not just a dawn; it is a precious chance to start over or begin anew.**

DAY 2

# THE CHALLENGE

**Read Matthew 4:12-25.**

*"Come, follow me," Jesus said (v. 19).*

**J**im Stanley never backed away from a challenge.

In high school during a football playoff game, the opposing players started talking trash before the kickoff, telling Stanley they were going to come after him. Sure enough, he finished the first play with his lip busted wide open. He refused to come out of the game and instead started taking out opposing players. The quarterback was the first to go. The running back was next, and then went his replacement, followed by the replacement's sub. Asked about the truth of that story shortly before he died at 77 in 2012, Stanley, a man of few words, simply said, "I don't know if there were four of them."

Stanley took on the challenge of coaching the Oklahoma State football team in 1973. The team had gone 6-5 in 1972, but that was the program's first winning season since a 6-4 mark in 1959. The Pokes had not beaten Oklahoma since 1966.

It was no coincidence that part of Stanley's pre-game ritual for his team always included watching a John Wayne movie. Like the hero on the screen, State's coach was described as "tough as a nail. Stoic as a statue. Just as a frontier lawman."

Russ Farthing, a walk-on who played for Stanley, said that Stanley's penchant for not saying much left the impression that "he was aloof. He looked mad." But the coach's players knew him quite differently, calling him "Bubba." "Great guy, great legacy," Farthing said. "Touched a lot of lives. Helped a lot of people. He took most of it to his grave because he wouldn't tell you."

Stanley forged a 35-31-2 record across six seasons in Stillwater. The Cowboys won a share of the Big Eight title in 1976, a season that included a 31-24 win over No. 5 Oklahoma. He then took on the challenge for nearly three decades of working in pro football.

Like the Oklahoma State athletic teams every time they take the field or the court, we are challenged daily. Life is a testing ground; God intentionally set it up that way. If we are to grow in character, confidence, and perseverance, and if we are to make a difference in the world, we must meet challenges head-on. Few things in life are as boring and as destructive to our sense of self-worth as a job that doesn't offer any challenges.

Our faith life is the same way. The moment we answered Jesus' call to "Come, follow me," we took on the most difficult challenge we will ever face. We are called to be holy by walking in Jesus' footsteps in a world that seeks to render our Lord irrelevant and his influence negligible. The challenge Jesus places before us is to put our faith and our trust in him and not in ourselves or the transitory values of the secular world.

Daily walking in Jesus' footsteps is a challenge, but the path takes us all the way right up to the gates of Heaven – and then right on through.

*He was an extremely tough individual and very hard-nosed.*
*-- Former OSU coach Bill Young on Jim Stanley and challenges*

**To accept Jesus as Lord is to joyfully take on the challenge of living a holy life in an unholy world.**

**THE CHALLENGE     5**

# SUPERSTITION

**Read Isaiah 2:6-16.**

*"They are full of superstitions from the East; . . . they bow down to the work of their hands" (vv. 6b, 8b).*

**F**rom drawing an X in the dirt before every at-bat to not dusting off a dirty jersey, the State baseball and softball players of 2009 had their superstitions and rituals.

Cowgirl third baseman Mariah Gearhart always touched the base in front of OSU's dugout -- whether it was first or third -- prior to warming up before an inning. If she slid during a game, she never dusted herself off; she also wouldn't allow anyone else to touch her jersey the rest of the game.

Baseball left fielder Neil Medchill drew an X in the dirt while he waited in the on-deck circle to bat. He then hit the barrel of his bat on the X to make the donut land right in the center. He also walked to the plate with his bat tucked under his arm.

Each time he warmed up between innings, shortstop Tom Belza made sure he once treated the ball like a football, stepping back and passing it to third baseman Tyrone Hambly. If pitcher Jared Starks had a bad game, he retired his undershirt. When he batted, first baseman Dean Green leaned the bat against his legs, adjusted his batting gloves, and pulled his helmet down tight -- before every pitch.

Cowgirl pitcher Anna Whiddon once told on her teammate, Katelyn Bright: "Whenever she's on base, she literally thinks that if she doesn't pick up dirt, something bad is going to happen."

The '09 softball team even had a team-wide ritual. Before each inning, the players all hit their bats together and did a little dance. In realization of the futility of superstition, they also prayed as a team before each game.

OSU baseball coach Frank Anderson suggested that the rituals had a place in that they helped his players "focus on what's at hand, rather than the crowd or people getting on you."

Superstitions can be quite benign. Nothing in the Bible warns us about the dangers inherent in refusing to wear a certain shirt or bumping bats together.

God is quite concerned, however, about superstition of a more serious nature such as using the occult to predict the future. Its danger for us is that we allow something other than God to take precedence in our lives; we in effect worship idols.

While most of us scoff at palm readers and psychics, we nevertheless risk being idol worshippers of a different sort. Just watch the frenzied reaction of fans when a movie star or a star football player shows up. Or consider how we often compromise what we know is right merely to save face or to gain favor in the workplace.

Superstition is the stuff of nonsense. Idol worshipping, however, is as real for us today as it was for the Israelites. It is also just as dangerous.

*I could tell you a bazillion, but some are dumber than others.*
*-- Mariah Gearhart on her softball superstitions*

**Superstition in the form of idol worship is alive**
**and well today, occurring anytime we venerate**
**anything other than God.**

# TEACHER'S PET

**Read John 3:1-16.**

*"[Nicodemus] came to Jesus at night and said, 'Rabbi, we know you are a teacher who has come from God'" (v. 2).*

Even the coach admitted the whole situation was "a little odd." The player was doing the teaching.

Todd Monken took over as Oklahoma State's offensive coordinator in February 2011 after Dana Holgorsen moved to West Virginia. The change in coordinators presented head coach Mike Gundy with a rather interesting problem. The team needed "to replicate the attack without the architect."

That is, the offense really didn't need to make any changes. After all, in 2010 OSU had ranked third nationally in total yardage and scoring. Much of that offensive talent returned, including one of the nation's best combinations in quarterback Brandon Weeden and wide receiver Justin Blackmon. Weeden had set OSU records in passing yards and touchdowns while Blackmon had led the nation in receiving and had won the Biletnikoff Award as college football's best receiver. The Cowboys went 11-2.

So having a new offensive coordinator step into that situation "was a little tricky." But Monken came to Stillwater with an attitude that was somewhat unusual for coaches, who are usually called upon to implement their systems to foster improvement. Instead, Monken "was willing to come in and work within our system," Gundy said. That "allowed us to make one guy adjust instead of making 60 people adjust."

It also meant Monken had to go to school on the Poke offense -- and the best teacher was right on hand. It was Breeden. "He's gotta be involved in the teaching process," Gundy said, "because he knows more about [the offense] than anybody in the building."

In an unusual twist, the coach became the student and the player became the teacher. It turned out quite well. In 2011, OSU led the Big 12 and ranked second nationally in scoring offense and passing offense. The team was third in total offense.

You can read this book, break 90 on the golf course, and be successful at your job because somebody taught you. And as you learn, you become the teacher yourself. You teach your children how to play Monopoly and how to drive a car. You show rookies the ropes at the office and teach baseball's basics to Little Leaguers.

This pattern of learning and then teaching includes your spiritual life also. Somebody taught you about Jesus, and this, too, you must pass on. Jesus came to teach a truth the religious teachers and the powerful of his day did not want to hear. Little has changed in that regard, as the world today often reacts with scorn and disdain to Jesus' message.

Nothing, not even death itself, could stop Jesus from teaching his lesson of life and salvation. So should nothing stop you from teaching life's most important lesson: Jesus saves.

*We're kind of piecing it together.*
*-- Todd Monken on learning the OSU offense*

**In life, you learn and then you teach,**
**which includes learning and teaching about Jesus,**
**the most important lesson of all.**

# PAY YOUR RESPECTS

**Read Mark 8:31-38.**

*"He then began to teach them that the Son of Man must suffer many things and be rejected by the elders, chief priests and teachers of the law, and that he must be killed" (v. 31).*

Pat Jones coached some of the greatest players in the history of college football. He was adamant, however, that the player whom he respected the most was one who lost his starting job.

Jones was the Cowboys' head coach from 1984-1994. He won 62 games; from 1984-88, OSU went 44-15, at the time the greatest run in the program's history. He coached the likes of Barry Sanders, Thurman Thomas, Rusty Hilger, Hart Lee Dykes, Leslie O'Neal, Ernest Anderson, and Gerald Hudson, all great players. But the player he respected the most was Ronnie Williams.

As a sophomore, Williams was the starting quarterback in 1985. The team went 8-4 and played in the Gator Bowl. In 1986, though, the Pokes had to rally to beat Southwestern Louisiana by a point and lost to Tulsa. Williams was throwing too many interceptions. "I had seen all the turnovers I wanted to see," Jones said.

When Houston jumped out to a 21-3 lead in a first half that featured another interception, Jones made a decision. "We loved [Williams], but he was turnover-prone and we had [true freshman Mike] Gundy in the wings. We needed to get Mike going," the head coach said. So at halftime, Jones told Gundy he was in.

And Williams' reaction? He first sailed his helmet across the locker room, but after that, Jones said, "Ronnie handled it about as well as a man could handle it." The head coach knew his decision could have wrecked the team, but Williams earned everyone's respect. "Ronnie's reaction was one of the most powerful events the whole time I was there," Jones said.

The boss Poke moved Williams to receiver, and he was immediately in the rotation. He went on to play tight end in the NFL.

The late Rodney Dangerfield made a good living with a comedic repertoire that was basically only countless variations on one punch line: "I don't get no respect." Dangerfield was successful because he struck a chord with his audience. Like the late comedian, we all seek a measure of respect in our lives. We want the respect, the esteem, and the regard we feel we have earned.

But more often than not we don't get it. Still, we shouldn't feel too badly; we're in good company. In the ultimate example of disrespect, Jesus – the very Son of God -- was treated as the worst type of criminal. He was arrested, bound, scorned, ridiculed, spit upon, tortured, condemned, and executed.

God allowed his son to undergo such treatment because of his high regard and his love for each one of us. We are respected by almighty God! Could anyone else's respect really matter?

*Of all the guys that went through that program in the 16 years I was there, there was nobody I had more respect for than Ronnie Williams.*
*-- Pat Jones*

**You may not get the respect you deserve,**
**but at least nobody's spitting on you**
**and driving nails into you as they did to Jesus.**

# FOR THE FUN OF IT

**Read Nehemiah 8:1-12.**

*"Do not grieve, for the joy of the Lord is your strength"*
*(v. 10c).*

Evan Howell had so much fun he called his parents as soon as he got back to Stillwater. His teammates had a pretty good time, too, as they blasted Oklahoma.

Bob Simmons' Cowboys won their first six games of the 1997 season, one of them a 42-16 waxing of Texas, before a pair of heartbreaking overtime losses ended the run. Next up, was Bedlam and a chance to restore some magic to the season.

And magic it was. The 25th-ranked Cowboys hopped on the backs of their defense as they had all season and stomped the Sooners 30-7 in Norman. The State defenders forced six turnovers and held OU to 198 total yards, only 82 the last half. OSU led 13-7 at halftime, and as free safety/wideout R.W. McQuarters said, "We came out in the second half and just hit them in the mouth and put pressure on them. We knew they would fold."

Freshman quarterback Tony Lindsay set a Cowboy record by throwing his eighth and ninth touchdown passes of the season, breaking Mike Gundy's mark. He joined Simmons and senior cornerback Kevin Williams in being hoisted onto the shoulders of their fellow Cowboys in a postgame celebration at midfield.

Nobody had more fun or a bigger smile, though, than Howell. A reserve defensive back, the sophomore got his most extensive playing time of the season when Ricky Thompson was injured. He responded with a fumble recovery and an interception.

Howell's most urgent plan was to call his parents in Monroe, La., as soon as he hit Stillwater. He admitted he would be excited to talk to them and tell them how he played, though getting any words out would be difficult since he couldn't stop smiling.

An erroneous stereotype of the Christian lifestyle has emerged, that of a dour, sour-faced person always on the prowl to sniff out fun and frivolity and shut it down. "Somewhere, sometime, somebody's having fun – and it's got to stop!" Many understand this to be the mandate that governs the Christian life.

But even the Puritans, from whom that American stereotype largely comes, had parties, wore bright colors, and allowed their children to play games.

God's attitude toward fun is clearly illustrated by Nehemiah's instructions to the Israelites after Ezra had read them God's commandments. They broke out into tears because they had failed God, but Nehemiah told them not to cry but to eat, drink, and be merry instead. Go have fun, believers! Celebrate God's goodness and forgiveness!

This is still our mandate today because a life spent in awareness of God's presence is all about celebrating, rejoicing, and enjoying God's countless gifts, especially salvation in Jesus Christ. To live for Jesus is to truly know the fun in living.

*Just play. Have fun. Enjoy the game.*

-- *Michael Jordan*

**What on God's wonderful Earth can be more fun
that living for Jesus?**

# A RIPE OLD AGE

**Read Psalm 92.**

*"[The righteous] will still bear fruit in old age, they will stay fresh and green, proclaiming, 'The Lord is upright'"* *(vv. 14-15).*

After the 2012 season, the grand old man of Oklahoma State sports stepped down.

James Wadley coached men's tennis at State for forty years. When he retired, he was the longest tenured coach in the school's athletic history. He thus outlasted the OSU coach he respected above all others, Henry Iba, by four seasons.

Wadley gave up his high school job and took over the State tennis program in 1972 with a salary of $4,500. Sportswriter Berry Tramel said the move resulted in a pay cut; to make ends meet, Wadley got a part-time job working at an apartment complex's laundry. State head football coach Mike Gundy was 5 years old. Richard Nixon was the President. Writer John Klein said more than 60 head coaches in all sports had been hired at OSU since Wadley took over the tennis program.

Wadley had been planning his retirement for a while. In 2009, he told athletic director Mike Holder he wanted to coach another three years. The time had come. "I'm ready to go," Wadley said. "It isn't as much fun as it used to be, so it is probably time for me."

Those forty seasons went by fast, though, for the veteran coach. "That's what happens when you are having as much fun as I've had," he said. "I loved the job. I like college athletics and I like college towns. So, this was perfect for me."

Wadley coached nearly 1,000 dual matches and won 664 of them. His Cowboy teams won twelve conference titles and made seventeen trips to the NCAA Tournament. He was the conference coach of the year thirteen times.

Wadley said retirement probably wouldn't be that different for him. "My wife thinks I'm retired already," he said. "I wear shorts to work and have a lot of time off in the summer."

James Wadley's forty years as a head coach certainly qualified him as OSU's grand old man. He retired gracefully, but in our youth-obsessed culture, we generally don't like to admit – even to ourselves – that we're not as young as we used to be.

So we keep plastic surgeons in business, dye our hair, buy cases of those miracle wrinkle-reducing creams, and redouble our efforts in the gym. Sometimes, though, we just have to face up to the truth the mirror tells us: We're getting older every day.

It's really all right, though, because aging and old age are part of the natural cycle of our lives, which was God's idea in the first place. God's conception of the golden years, though, doesn't include unlimited close encounters with a rocking chair and nothing more. God expects us to serve him as we are able all the days of our life. Those who serve God flourish no matter their age because the energizing power of God is in them.

*He's older than Methuselah.*
*-- OSU athletic director Mike Holder on James Wadley*

**Servants of God don't ever retire; they keep working until they get the ultimate promotion.**

# LANGUAGE BARRIER

**Read Acts 2:1-21.**

*"Divided tongues, as of fire, appeared among them, and a tongue rested on each of them. All of them were filled with the Holy Spirit and began to speak in other languages, as the Spirit gave them ability" (vv. 3-4 NRSV).*

**W**hile his teammates had fun in Dallas, Parker Graham found himself in an airport shuttle van speeding toward the wrong city and getting cussed out in a foreign language.

The Cowboys closed out the 2012 season with a trip to Dallas for the Heart of Dallas Bowl on Jan. 1 against the Purdue Boilermakers. As with any bowl game, the trip was a mixture of fun in the city and business on the practice field. Quarterback Clint Chelf declared that head coach Mike Gundy "said it best when he was talking to us the other day that it's all fun, but it makes it a lot more fun when you win the game."

Graham, a junior starting tackle, missed some of the fun when he found himself stranded by the winter weather. The native of Webb City, Mo., had trouble flying into the Dallas area. When he finally did land, he had even more problems.

As center Evan Epstein recounted, Graham took a shuttle into the city but soon realized he wasn't in Dallas. He texted Epstein, who is from McKinney, Texas, and knows the area, and said he was in Bedford. The driver was taking him to Fort Worth.

When Graham protested, "the driver starting cussing at [him] in French," Epstein said. Graham was a member of the All-Big 12 Academic Team and speaks French. He had no problem letting the driver know exactly how things stood.

Graham eventually arrived at the right hotel in time to get to a team meeting, as Epstein put it, "in the wrong outfit with a plate of food because he missed lunch."

As Parker Graham's encounter with a driver who thought he could get away with insulting the player by speaking in French, language differences frequently -- if not usually -- erect a barrier to understanding. Recall your overseas vacation or your call to a tech support number when you got someone who spoke English but didn't understand it.

Like many other aspects of life, faith has its jargon that can sometimes hinder understanding. Sanctification, justification, salvation, Advent, Communion with its symbolism of eating flesh and drinking blood – these and many other words have specific meanings to Christians that may be incomprehensible, confusing, and downright daunting to the newcomer or the seeker.

But the heart of Christianity's message centers on words that require no explanation: words such as hope, joy, love, purpose, and community. Their meanings are universal because people the world over seek them in their lives. Nobody speaks that language better than Jesus.

*Kindness is the universal language that all people understand.*
*-- Legendary Florida A&M Coach Jake Gaither*

**Jesus speaks across all language barriers**
**because his message of hope and meaning**
**resounds with people everywhere.**

# WHOLEHEARTEDLY

**Read 1 Samuel 13:1-14.**

*"The Lord has sought out a man after his own heart" (v. 14).*

After suffering a heartbreaking loss, the Cowboys of 1976 showed how much heart they had by rallying to win the Big Eight championship.

It has been called "one of [Oklahoma State's] most cherished football seasons." The Cowboys of 1976 went 8-3, 6-2 in league play and earned a share of the school's only Big Eight title. They crushed Brigham Young 49-21 in the Tangerine Bowl.

The Cowboys fielded one of their most talented teams ever. Defensive tackle Phillip Dokes, punter Cliff Parsley, offensive linemen Derrel Gofourth and Ron Baker, and running back Robert Turner were drafted by the NFL. Eventually, twelve players off that '76 team were drafted by the pros.

The most decorated player on the team was junior running back Terry Miller. He was a two-time Big Eight Player of the Year and a two-time All-America and is the second-leading rusher in OSU history behind Thurman Thomas.

Only one of the most heartbreaking losses in school history prevented the Pokes from winning the title outright. They led Colorado 10-6 with less than two minutes remaining. On fourth down from the State 18, a Buffalo pass was intercepted in the end zone. Instead of taking a knee, the player tried to run it out and fumbled at the 1. Colorado recovered and scored for the win.

The Cowboys refused to be disheartened. Rather, they drew closer together and grew more determined. One week after the loss, they beat two-time defending national champion Oklahoma 31-24. A week later, they rallied from a 16-0 third-quarter deficit to beat Missouri 20-19. They won six of seven games after the Colorado heartbreaker.

"I thought we were one of the best teams in the nation at the end of the year," said Jim Stanley, the team's head coach. The squad certainly had the collective heart of a champion.

We all face defeat as the '76 Cowboys did. Sometimes, even though we fight with all we have, we lose.

At some time, you probably have admitted you were whipped no matter how much it hurt. Always in your life, though, you have known that you would fight for some things with all your heart and never give them up: your family, your country, your friends, your core beliefs.

God should be on that list too. God seeks men and women who will never turn their back on him because they are people after God's own heart. That is, they will never betray God with their unbelief; they will never lose their childlike trust in God; they will never cease to love God with all their heart.

They are lifetime members of God's team; it's a mighty good one to be on, but it takes heart.

*That [Colorado loss] helped them to grow and become more of a one-heart team.*
*-- Quarterback Charlie Weatherbie of the '76 team*

**God's team requires the heart of a champion.**

# MEMORY LOSS

**Read 1 Corinthians 11:17-29.**

*"[D]o this in remembrance of me" (v. 24).*

I'm going to remember this when I'm 70," screamed 21-year-old wide receiver Rashaun Woods. "This" was an unbelievable, never-to-be-forgotten defeat of Oklahoma.

Little about the 2001 football season turned out as Cowboy fans, coaches, and players expected. With new head coach Les Miles in Stillwater, talk in the preseason was of a bowl game. Instead, OSU showed up for Bedlam with a 3-7 record.

On the other hand, the Sooners from Norman were ranked No 4 and had their sites set on the Big 12 championship game and a berth in the Rose Bowl for the national title. They were four-touchdown favorites on their home turf.

Woods isn't alone in remembering what happened on Nov. 25, 2001. In a "stunning, monumental victory," OSU beat Oklahoma 16-13. One writer called it the biggest win in school history.

Playing with a dislocated thumb that he had to pop back into place, freshman quarterback Josh Fields led the Cowboys to a field goal and a touchdown in the last seven minutes of the game that brought the Pokes back from a 13-6 deficit. The game-winning drive covered 65 yards in six plays with Fields "showing uncommon cool in a red-hot moment." The touchdown came on a 14-yard toss to Woods with 1:36 to play. The score was set up by a 31-yard reception by receiver Terrance Davis-Bryant.

# COWBOYS

The Sooners had some time after the kickoff, but four straight incompletions was all they could muster. The Cowboy defense was stout all day, allowing Oklahoma only 220 yards total offense and zero yards rushing with sacks factored in.

"I thought all along we had a chance in this game," Miles said. [Our guys] felt they had a chance to win." That put them in a distinct minority until they went out and gave Oklahoma State fans and themselves a memory for the ages.

Memory makes us who we are. Whether our memories appear as pleasant reverie or unnerving nightmares, they shape us and to a large extent determine both our actions and our reactions. Alzheimer's is so terrifying because it steals our memory from us, and in the process we lose ourselves. We disappear.

The greatest tragedy of our lives is that God remembers. In response to that photographic memory, he condemns us for our sin. Paradoxically, the greatest joy of our lives is that God remembers. In response to that memory, he came as Jesus to wash even the memory of our sins away.

God uses memory as a tool through which we encounter revival. At the Last Supper, Jesus instructed his disciples and us to remember. In sharing this unique meal with fellow believers and remembering Jesus and his actions, we meet Christ again, not just as a memory but as an actual living presence. To remember is to keep our faith alive.

*This is something OSU fans and these players will remember forever.*
*-- OSU left guard Jeff Machado on Bedlam 2001*

**Because we remember Jesus,**
**God will not remember our sins.**

# IN THE BAD TIMES

**Read Philippians 1:3-14.**

*"What has happened to me has really served to advance
the gospel. . . . Because of my chains, most of the brothers
in the Lord have been encouraged to speak the word of
God more courageously and fearlessly" (vv. 12, 14).*

**P**aul Hansen's early days at OSU were not exactly the best of
times for his family and him.

Hansen took over a struggling Cowboy men's basketball program in 1979. He was described as "an affable man with thinning
brown hair, small eyes, a hearing aid and a startled laugh." He
needed all the affability and laughter he could dredge up in the
bad times that were his first season at OSU.

His family had barely settled into their new home before it was
burglarized. "We lived square in the middle of the highest crime
area in Oklahoma City and were never touched," Hansen said.
"We get into white, conservative America, and we're ripped off!"

A few weeks later, a pickup truck nailed one of the Hansens'
dogs. The pooch recovered, only to be run over again, fatally.
The other dog simply disappeared, presumably stolen.

The bad times carried over onto Hansen's first team. The star
player, Matt Clark, went down for the year with a knee injury.
In practice, Don Youmans, OSU's top rebounder from the season
before, slapped the ball off the glass and in the process damaged
two tendons in a thumb. Out for nine games. Seven weeks later,

two frontcourt starters went down with bad grades.

The Cowboys finished 10-17. Then Hansen started feeling bad at a 1980 preseason practice. Assistant coach Wayne Ballard asked, "Coach, have you looked at your eyes lately?" They were yellow. He had hepatitis and spent four weeks in bed.

In the second game of the season, though, junior guard Eddie Harmon nailed a 45-shot prayer at the buzzer for his only field goal of the game. It beat Louisville, the defending national champs.

The Pokes had a good time going 18-9 that season.

Loved ones die. You're downsized. Your biopsy looks cancerous. Your spouse could be having an affair. Hard, tragic times are as much a part of life as breath.

This applies to Christians too. Christianity is not the equivalent of a Get-out-of-Jail-Free card, granting us a lifelong exemption from either the least or the worst pain the world has to offer. While Jesus promises us he will be there to lead us through the valleys, he never promises that we will not enter them.

The question therefore becomes how you handle the bad times. You can buckle to your knees in despair and cry, "Why me?" Or you can hit your knees and ask God, "What do I do with this?"

Setbacks and tragedies are opportunities to reveal and to develop true character and abiding faith. Your faithfulness -- and not your skipping merrily along through life without pain -- is what reveals the depth of your love for God.

*Hey, I'm a happy guy. Shucks, those things are just going to happen.*
*-- Paul Hansen on his misfortunes at OSU early on*

**Faithfulness to God requires faith even in --**
**especially in -- the bad times.**

# TRICK PLAYS

**Read Acts 19:11-20.**

*"The evil spirit answered them, 'Jesus I know, and I know about Paul, but who are you?'" (v. 15)*

The Cowboys were struggling against Kansas State until they threw in a little trick to their kick.

OSU and the 22nd-ranked Wildcats were deadlocked at 21 in the third quarter in Stillwater on Oct. 11, 2003. The Cats had all the momentum, though, after scoring a touchdown and then limiting State to a field-goal try. That's when special teams coordinator Joe DeForest decided it was time for a little trickery.

DeForest had been somewhat impatiently waiting all season to try a trick play. At the start of every special teams practice since August, he had had kicker Luke Phillips and holder Sky Rylant practice a fake field goal. DeForest had originally intended to use it in the season opener against Nebraska, but the right situation never came up. Now in the sixth game of the season, that situation arose when K State gave him the look he needed.

The Wildcats crowded the interior of the line with two jumpers right behind in an attempt to block the 48-yard attempt. The contain for a running play was not there. DeForest made the call.

Phillips had never carried the ball either in high school or college, but the duo executed the trick play perfectly. Rylant took the snap from Jacob Dressen and flipped the ball behind his head to Phillips, who sprinted down the wide-open right side. The kicker admitted that when he first saw all that unmanned turf, he had visions of going all the way. The secondary closed quickly, though, and Phillips got out of bounds but not before he picked up 11 yards and a first down.

Three plays later, Josh Fields threw a TD pass to wide receiver Gabe Lindsay. It was the beginning of 17 straight Cowboy points that produced a 38-21 lead. A late K State rally fell short as OSU won 38-34, thanks in large part to a perfectly executed trick play.

Scam artists are everywhere — and they love trick plays. An e-mail encourages you to send money to some foreign country to get rich. That guy at your front door offers to resurface your driveway at a ridiculously low price. A TV ad promises a pill to help you lose weight without diet or exercise.

You've been around; you check things out before deciding. The same approach is necessary with spiritual matters, too, because false religions and bogus Christian denominations abound. The key is what any group does with Jesus. Is he the son of God, the ruler of the universe, and the only way to salvation? If not, then what the group espouses is something other than the true Word of God.

The good news about Jesus does indeed sound too good to be true, but the only catch is that there is no catch. When it comes to salvation through Jesus Christ, there's no trick lurking in the fine print. There's just the truth, right there for you to see.

*After the fake, the success of our offense was very evident.*
*-- Les Miles on the game-changing trick play vs. K State*

**God's promises through Jesus sound too good to be true, but the only catch is that there is no catch.**

# STRANGE BUT TRUE

**Read Philippians 2:1-11.**

*"And being found in appearance as a man, he humbled himself and became obedient to death – even death on a cross!" (v. 7)*

It's strange but it is most certainly true: A basketball injury may well have cost Thurman Thomas the Heisman Trophy.

Thomas, of course, is a Cowboy and a college football legend. From 1984-87, he amassed 4,595 yards rushing, the most in school history. He was a first-team All-America in 1985 and in 1987. He was elected to the College Football Hall of Fame in 2008 and joins Terry Miller and Barry Sanders as the only three OSU football players to have their jersey number retired.

Thomas had a breakout season as a sophomore in '85, rushing for 1,553 yards, fourth best in the country. He finished tenth in the Heisman-Trophy voting. He thus entered the '86 season with a lot of momentum, name recognition, and publicity. He was a star and a leading Heisman contender; if not in '86, certainly as a senior in '87, the award was his to seize.

In June, though, Thomas injured his knee in a pickup basketball game. As head coach Pat Jones put it, "He just went up for a shot, wasn't even touched, and a ligament popped."

When the doctors opened up Thomas' knee, they decided not to do anything. The opinion was that the ligament was one he could live and play football without. "It sounds bad, but if your quads are strong enough, you can play," Jones said.

Thomas had what was for him a down year in 1986 with 774 yards. He bounced back with a vengeance his senior season and finished third nationally with 1,613 yards rushing. The subpar junior year cost him all the momentum he had built up his first two seasons, however. He finished seventh in the Heisman voting.

Some things in life are so strange their existence can't really be explained. How else can we account for the delay in getting a major college football playoff, tattoos, curling, tofu, and the behavior of teenagers? Isn't it strange that today we have more ways to stay in touch with each other yet are losing the intimacy of personal contact?

And how strange is God's plan to save us? Think a minute about what God did. He could have come roaring down, destroying and blasting everyone whose sinfulness offended him, which, of course, is pretty much all of us. Then he could have brushed off his hands, nodded the divine head, and left a scorched planet in his wake. All in a day's work.

Instead, God came up with a totally novel plan: He would save the world by becoming a human being, letting himself be humiliated, tortured, and killed, thus establishing a kingdom of justice and righteousness that will last forever.

It's a strange way to save the world – but it's true.

*[1986] was a hard-luck year for Thurman. A bee even stung him inside his helmet when we played at Houston.*
*-- Pat Jones on the season that may have cost Thomas the Heisman*

**It's strange but true: God allowed himself
to be killed on a cross to save the world.**

# A LONG SHOT

**Read Matthew 9:9-13.**

*"[Jesus] saw a man named Matthew sitting at the tax collector's booth. 'Follow me,' he told him, and Matthew got up and followed him" (v. 9).*

One sure indicator that a recruit is a long shot comes when a coach answers a question about him by muddling his answer to camouflage it. That's what happened with Devin Davis.

At an Oklahoma State recruiting meeting when Davis was in high school, offensive line coach Joe Wickline told the other coaches he wanted to offer a scholarship to this big kid from Nacogdoches, Texas. The coaches' first concern was who their competition was, so immediately someone asked, "Who else is recruiting him?" Wickline described the moment as "one of those situations where you 'almost cough under your breath' to camouflage your response." What was his troublesome answer? "Nobody."

Oklahoma State was considering offering a scholarship to a player that absolutely no one was recruiting? That's right. In fact, Wickline joked that Davis' options were OSU or the army.

And it's not like no one had heard of Davis. A member of the Nacogdoches staff alerted Wickline to Davis, saying, "This guy is going to be a really good player and he is a beautiful kid." Wickline asked the coach how many people he had said the same thing to, and he replied, "I told everybody." No major school bit, however, because Davis had the frame of a big man but had yet to really grow up.

Oklahoma State did, though. Head coach Mike Gundy went along with Wickline's wish. "I have faith in our coaches," he said. Davis arrived in Stillwater in 2011 and was redshirted. He hit the weights and played tackel at 6'5" and 298 pounds in 2012. This long shot was penciled in as the starting left tackel in 2013 until a pre-season knee inury sidelined him for the year.

Like Devin Davis, Matthew the tax collector was a long shot. In his case, he was an unlikely person to be a confidant of the Son of God. While we may not get all warm and fuzzy about the IRS, our government's revenue agents are nothing like Matthew and his ilk. He bought a franchise, paying the Roman Empire for the privilege of extorting, bullying, and stealing everything he could from his own people. Tax collectors of the time were "despicable, vile, unprincipled scoundrels."

And yet, Jesus said only two words to this lowlife: "Follow me." Jesus knew that this long shot would make an excellent disciple.

It's the same with us. While we may not be quite as vile as Matthew was, none of us can stand before God with our hands clean and our hearts pure. We are all impossibly long shots to enter God's Heaven. That is, until we do what Matthew did: get up and follow Jesus.

*He had the worst feet. He was undersized. He wasn't that heavy or real strong.*
    *-- Tackle Calvin Barnett on his long-shot roommate, Devin Davis*

**Jesus changes us  from being long shots
to enter God's Kingdom to being sure things.**

# NOT WHAT THEY SEEM

**Read Habakkuk 1:2-11.**

*"Why do you make me look at injustice? Why do you tolerate wrong? Destruction and violence are before me; there is strife, and conflict abounds" (v. 3).*

Oklahoma State's golf team appeared to be in trouble as they headed into a sudden-death playoff for the national championship. Ah, but things were not what they seemed.

In 1995, for the first time in the 98-year history of the NCAA's golf tournament, two teams -- the Cowboys and the Stanford Cardinal -- wound up in a tie when regulation play ended. It was fitting. The Pokes were ranked No. 1, and Stanford, the defending champion -- led by freshman Tiger Woods -- was No. 2.

The Cowboys finished with a charge to force the playoff. Senior Alan Bratton, the 1994 NCAA Co-Player of the Year, birdied his last three holes. All-American Trip Kuehne also birdied the last hole to complete a surge that saw the team erase an eight-shot Stanford lead over the last nine holes. When Woods missed a birdie putt on the final hole -- sudden death playoff.

That's when the Cowboys seemed to be in real trouble. The format called for the two teams to send five players to the 18th hole with the best four scores counting. But OSU didn't have a fifth player. Sophomore Leif Westerberg had left immediately after the final round to fly to England for the British Amateur.

State head coach Mike Holder wasn't concerned. "We had made

the travel plans in early April, so I had no regrets" about winding up a player short, he said. Neither were his players worried. Their confidence was the product of a training regimen that included 6 a.m. aerobics classes and regular practices in bad weather. "Lots of folks say [Holder] runs a boot camp," Kuehne said. "But we love it and we're great friends."

Bratton and junior Kris Cox nailed birdie putts while Stanford could manage only four pars. As it turned out, the Pokes weren't short-handed at all; what they were was national champions.

Sometimes in life things aren't what they seem. In our violent and convulsive times, we must confront the possibility of a new reality: that we are helpless in the face of anarchy; that injustice, destruction, and violence are pandemic in and symptomatic of our modern age. Anarchy seems to be winning, and the system of standards, values, and institutions we have cherished appears to be crumbling while we watch.

But we should not be deceived or disheartened. God is in fact the arch-enemy of chaos, the creator of order and goodness and the architect of all of history. God is in control. We often misinterpret history as the record of mankind's accomplishments -- which it isn't -- rather than the unfolding of God's plan -- which it is. That plan has a clearly defined end: God will make everything right. In that day things will be what they seem.

*What [Coach Mike Holder] makes us do allowed us to conquer the odds.*
*-- Trip Kuehne on winning the playoff despite being shorthanded*

**The forces of good and decency often seem
helpless before evil's power, but don't be fooled:
God is in control and will set things right.**

# THANKS A LOT

**Read 1 Thessalonians 5:12-28.**

*"[G]ive thanks in all circumstances, for this is God's will for you in Christ Jesus" (v. 18).*

**K**ye Staley didn't have a fancy touchdown celebration planned. He just knelt and gave thanks to God.

On their way to the Big 12 championship in 2011, the Cowboys blew out Baylor 59-24 on Oct. 29 to up their record to 8-0. Late in the first quarter came a touchdown that was called "Oklahoma State's season-defining moment." Considering the outcome, the score wasn't anything important, but it left quarterback Brandon Weeden with chills and "epitomize[d] this team's version of the Cowboy Code -- unselfish play, heart and teamwork." With 4:37 to go in the first quarter, Staley caught an 18-yard pass from Weeden for his first-ever college touchdown.

Staley came to Stillwater in 2008 and was redshirted. During 2009's fall camp, he pretty much destroyed his knee. Nerve damage left Staley's leg and foot numb. Doctors wondered if he'd ever walk again, let alone play football. So he limped away from football. "Football had always been a big part of me," Staley said, "but I had to look out for myself."

Still, football kept calling him back, and in 2010 he returned to the game. In the spring game of 2011, he led all rushers with 55 yards. Heading into the Baylor game, he had caught eight passes for 57 yards and had one rush.

During the week, offensive coordinator Todd Monken put in a play designed to get Staley his first score. It worked to perfection. Staley was surprised at how wide open he was. "I looked around and said, 'Oh my goodness, I have to score this.'"

He did. In the end zone, he held the ball so long he thought he might draw a flag. Then he dropped to his knees. "[I] thanked the man above for blessing me for being able to get a touchdown finally and blessing me in so many ways -- being able to walk and being where I am right now," Staley said.

Thank you, Lord, for my cancer. Thank you, Lord, for my unemployment. Thank you, Lord, that my children are in trouble with the law. Is this what the Bible means when it tells us to always be thankful?

Of course not. Being a man of reasonably good sense, Paul didn't tell us to give thanks for everything that happens to us, but to give thanks to God even when bad things occur. The joy we know in our soul through Jesus, the prayers we offer to God, and the gratitude we feel for the blessings that are in our lives even in the midst of distress – these don't fluctuate with our mood or our circumstances.

Failure to thank God implies we believe we alone are responsible for the good things in our lives. Such an arrogance relegates God to the fringes of our lives. An attitude of gratitude keeps God right where he belongs in our lives: at the heart and soul.

*The more you give thanks, the more you find things to be thankful for.*
*-- Weightlifter Bob Hoffman*

**No matter what, we can always be thankful
for God's presence in our lives.**

# PAYBACK

**Read Matthew 5:38-42.**

*"I tell you, Do not resist an evil person. If someone strikes you on the right cheek, turn to him the other also" (v. 39).*

**C**owboy quarterback Bobby Reid found himself harassed by a vociferous "kind-of-drunk" fan. He exacted his revenge in the best way possible: by having the game of his life.

Against Kansas on Oct. 14, 2006, OSU's sophomore quarterback lost a fumble in the third quarter. The Jayhawks took advantage of the miscue to kick a field goal and grab a 17-0 lead. On the sideline as he waited for the next State possession, Reid unaccountably found himself listening to a loud-mouthed Kansas fan sitting behind the Cowboy bench. Reid described the man as "kind of chubby" and "kind of drunk." The heckler shouted, "You're rattled! You've got no composure!"

At the time, his harsh critique seemed to apply to the entire State team, not just to its quarterback. Over the next 21 minutes, though, Reid threw five touchdown passes, four of them to wide receiver Adarius Bowman, and scored another on a 29-yard run. He passed for 411 yards, just shy of Mike Gundy's school record of 429 yards. He added 46 yards rushing; his total offense of 457 broke Gundy's school record.

Kansas simply couldn't stop the Reid-to-Bowman circus. The junior wide receiver caught thirteen passes and set a single-game school record with 300 yards.

Reid first hit Bowman with a 54-yard bomb. After Bruce Redden recovered his own onside kick, Reid pulled off his 29-yard TD run. The Jayhawks went three-and-out, and Reid found Bowman again for a touchdown. In 3:41, OSU had scored three times and led 21-17. The Cowboys wound up with 603 yards and a 42-32 win. At one point, Reid took a moment to run behind the Cowboy bench and confront his critic. The man had nothing to say.

The very nature of an intense rivalry in college sports is that the loser will seek payback for the defeat of the season before. But what about in life when somebody's done you wrong; is it time to get even?

The problem with revenge in real-life is that it isn't as clear-cut as a scoreboard like that in the State-KU game of 2006. Life is so messy that any attempt at revenge is often inadequate or, worse, backfires and injures you.

As a result, you remain gripped by resentment and anger, which hurts you and no one else. You poison your own happiness while that other person goes blithely about her business. The only way someone who has hurt you can keep hurting you is if you're a willing participant.

But it doesn't have to be that way. Jesus ushered in a new way of living when he taught that we are not to seek revenge for personal wrongs and injuries. Let it go and go on with your life. What a relief!

*I saw him sitting down. He wouldn't look at me.*
*-- Bobby Reid on paying back his 'kind of drunk' heckler*

**Resentment and anger over a wrong injures you,**
**so forget it -- just as Jesus taught.**

# THE BLAME GAME

### Read Genesis 3:1-13.

*"The man said, 'The woman . . . gave me some fruit from the tree, and I ate it.' . . . The woman said, 'The serpent deceived me, and I ate'" (vv. 12, 13b).*

**O**SU head coach Pat Jones was ready to take the blame for what happened late in a game, but the opposing coach beat him to it.

The Cowboys of 1987 went 10-2 including a thrilling 35-33 defeat of West Virginia in the Sun Bowl. The squad finished the season ranked No. 11 in the country.

If nothing else that team was loaded in the backfield where two future hall of famers – senior Thurman Thomas and sophomore Barry Sanders – plied their wares. Moreover, Jones said, "Those guys were so talented that people probably don't realize how good the backs behind them were. We could have lined up Vernon Brown and Mitch Nash and done really well."

Thurman and Sanders combined for 318 yards rushing in the 49-17 bulldozing of Kansas on Nov. 14. Jones said of the game, "The score didn't do justice to how lopsided the matchup was."

The head Cowboy did what he could to hold the score down. Late in the game, Kansas scored a meaningless touchdown, and the kicking team trotted onto the field. Too late, Jones realized Sanders, an All-American kick returner that season, was on the field. He didn't want Sanders out there risking an injury.

Special teams coach George Walstad told his boss not to worry, that Kansas wouldn't kick it to Sanders anyway. The Jayhawk kicker tried to squib it but hit a line shot that hopped once right to Sanders. He took it 99 yards for a touchdown.

A mortified Jones apologized to the Kansas head coach at midfield after the game, but the coach would have none of it. He told Jones not to worry, that it was his team's fault for kicking to Sanders in the first place.

Much in our society has changed since that autumn afternoon in 1987 when the KU head coach wasn't willing to pass the buck. Today, we live in an age when many of us assume responsibility for something only when it goes right. Otherwise, we cast about for somebody else to blame; it's never *our* fault.

The blame game has its limits in our lives. It may work quite well with doting parents, overworked teachers in crowded classrooms, resigned spouses too beaten down to argue, or careless managers just looking to keep their job. Shifting the blame to someone else will not work, however, when it comes to God.

We are on our own in our faith life. Adam and Eve's futile attempts to shift the blame for their disobedience -- Adam to Eve, Eve to the serpent -- illustrate the tragedy of trying to avoid responsibility before God. It didn't work then; it won't work now.

Before God, there are no victims. There are only those who -- of their own free will -- have followed or rejected Jesus.

*I never blame myself when I'm not hitting. I just blame the bat, and if it keeps up, I change bats.*

*-- Yogi Berra*

**No one else is to blame if any one of us fails
to accept Jesus Christ as a personal savior.**

# THOSE THINGS

### Read Luke 13:1-9.

*"Or those eighteen who died when the tower in Siloam fell on them -- do you think they were more guilty than all the others living in Jerusalem? I tell you, no!" (vv 4, 5a)*

It was just one of those things, but it cost OSU's Jordan Oliver a national championship.

Oliver completed his senior season of 2012-13 as one of the most dominant wrestlers in the storied history of the Oklahoma State program. He went 37-0 and did not surrender a single takedown all season. He was State's thirteenth four-time All-America and wrestled to a 126-6 record at OSU. The season and Oliver's collegiate career ended in Des Moines with his second national title. Except for one of those things, it would have been his third.

After a 29-0 season and a national title as a sophomore in 2010-11, Jordan was a dominant 28-1 heading into the finals of the NCAA championship in 2011-12. The match was a real battle, and for a moment, Oliver seemed to have won the title with a takedown at the edge of the mat that beat the buzzer. What resulted, however, was "an egregious no-call by the referee." Oliver was not awarded the points for the takedown, and he finished as the runner-up.

Oliver remained bitter about the bad break and used it as motivation for his senior season. "It's definitely not the outcome I wanted," he said. "There is no revenge, but I walked away with a fire to make sure that doesn't happen again."

# COWBOYS

Oliver and his coach, John Smith, analyzed what happened that resulted in the championship match being so close to begin with. They changed Oliver's attacking style to make it even more relentless, so, as Smith said, his ace would never again be in "the position of making the referee decide instead of making it decisive on the scoreboard."

As the record shows, Oliver was never in that position again.

Like Jordan Oliver, you've probably had a few of "those things" in your own life: bad breaks that occur without regard to justice, morality, or fair play. You wonder if everything in life is random with events determined by a chance roll of some cosmic dice. Is there really somebody scripting all this with logic and purpose?

Yes, there is; God is the author of everything.

We know how it all began; we even know how it all will end. It's in God's book. The part we play in God's kingdom, though, is in the middle, and that part is still being revealed. The simple truth is that God's ways are different from ours. After all he's God and we are not. That's why we don't know what's coming our way, and why "those things" -- such as a ref's bad call against our team -- catch us by surprise and dismay us when they do occur.

What God asks of us is that we trust him. As the one – and the only one – in charge, he knows everything will be all right for those who follow Jesus.

*I have bitter feelings about that.*
*-- Jordan Oliver on the non-call in 2012*

**Life confounds us because, while we know the
end and the beginning of God's great story, we are
part of the middle, which God is still writing.**

# UNDERDOGS

**Read 1 Samuel 17:17-50.**

*"David said to the Philistine, . . . 'This day the Lord will hand you over to me, and I'll strike you down'" (vv. 45-46).*

Little David was pretty impressive against Goliath, but the Cowboys went him one better, slaying a pair of giants from Norman in consecutive seasons.

On Nov. 25, 2001, State upset fourth-ranked Oklahoma 16-13. (See Devotion No. 10.) The Sooners entered the game as four-touchdown favorites. The situation was somewhat better for the Cowboys for Bedlam 2002; they were only 14-point underdogs to the third-ranked Sooners.

This time, though, the underdog Cowboys didn't need a late touchdown to win as they had in '01. This time the giant killers from Stillwater "outplayed OU from start to finish -- offense, defense, special teams, coaching -- every phase." Beating OU for the fifth time in eight years, State won 38-28 in a game that wasn't as close as the score. "Two years in a row -- to spoil their national championship two years in a row -- that's unbelievable," crowed senior safety Chris Massey.

OSU scored touchdowns on four of its first five possessions. Across the line, the Sooners went three-and-out on four of their first five possessions. State led 28-6 at halftime and then scored on its first possession of the last half. When Oklahoma threatened to make a game of it at 35-21 early in the fourth quarter, sophomore quarterback Josh Fields led the Cowboys on a 14-play drive that took seven minutes off the clock. It ended with a field goal from Luke Phillips with four minutes left. Game over.

"What a great feeling," exulted senior defensive tackle Kevin Williams as he lingered on the field with other players, the OSU coaches, and some overjoyed fans long after the last whistle had blown and both goalposts had come down.

They were celebrating a giant killing. Again.

You probably don't gird your loins, pick up a slingshot and some smooth, round river rocks, and go out to battle ill-tempered giants regularly. You do, however, fight each day to make some economic and social progress and to keep the ones you love safe, sheltered, and protected. Armed only with your pluck, your knowledge, your wits, and your hustle, in many ways you are an underdog; the best you can hope for is that the world is indifferent. You need all the weapons you can get.

How about using the ultimate weapon David had: the absolute, unshakable conviction that when he tackled opposition of any size, he would prevail. He knew this because he did everything for God's glory and therefore God was in his corner. If you imitate David's lifestyle by glorifying God in everything you do, then God is there for you when you need him.

Who's the underdog then?

*You should always fear the underdogs.*
              *-- Oklahoma Gov.-elect Brad Henry after Bedlam 2002*

**Jesus Christ was the ultimate underdog;
all he did was change the world.**

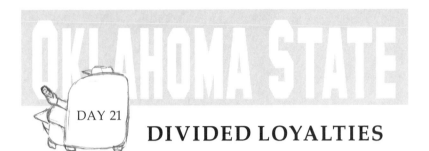

# DIVIDED LOYALTIES

**Read Matthew 6:1-24.**

*"No one can serve two masters" (v. 24a).*

Theirs was a house irretrievably divided -- until Zac came along. Bedlam around the Robinson household in suburban Denver was not an occasion for family unity and warmth. The husband, Rusty, attended OU from 1976-80 and had been a backup kicker with the Sooners. The wife, Myra, had attended OSU where she had been a Diamond Doll, a volunteer who did various odd jobs in support of the Cowboy baseball team. Daughters Katie Ann and Taylor joined Myra as State fans. Sons Zac and Chase joined Rusty in cheering for the Sooners.

During Bedlam telecasts, the family females watched the game on a downstairs TV while the family males did their whooping and hollering upstairs. Trash talk was the order of the day. As Zac remembered it, when the Cowboys scored, "My mom and sisters would do the wave and taunt us. . . . We were actually really mad."

This divided loyalty was especially prevalent during Zac's senior year of high school when he was being recruited by both State and OU. Mom and dad finally agreed Zac should make his decision without any pressure from either parent.

"I always dreamed of playing for OU," Zac said, but he liked what he saw in Stillwater. Ultimately the schemes of offensive co-ordinator Larry Fedora won him over. Zac signed with State.

That decision went a long way toward turning the Robinson

household into a family of Cowboys. The second week of the 2007 season locked up the transition. That's when Zac, a sophomore at State, got the starting nod from head coach Mike Gundy.

The Robinson household officially became a "house united" with universal support for the Cowboys. Rusty, the staunchest Sooner of them all, admitted, "I bleed orange."

The united family had much to cheer about over the next three seasons. In 2007, Zac set a new school record with 3,671 yards of offense, breaking the mark set by Josh Fields in 2002.

Like the Robinsons, you probably understand the stress that comes with divided loyalties. The Christian work ethic drives you to be successful. The world, however, often makes demands and presents images that conflict with your devotion to God: movies deride God; couples play musical beds in TV sitcoms; and TV dramas portray Christians as killers following God's orders.

It's Sunday morning and the office will be quiet or the golf course won't be crowded. What do you do when your heart and loyalties are pulled in two directions? Jesus knew of the struggle we face; that's why he spoke of not being able to serve "two masters," that we wind up serving one and despising the other. Put in terms of either serving God or despising God, the choice is stark and clear.

Your loyalty is to God -- always.

*It was definitely a house divided. But not anymore.*

*-- Rusty Robinson*

**God does not condemn you for being successful and enjoying popular culture, but your loyalty must lie first and foremost with him.**

# COMEBACK KIDS

**Read Luke 23:26-43.**

*"Jesus answered him, 'I tell you the truth, today you will be with me in paradise'" (v. 43).*

There was every reason to believe that Oklahoma State's season was heading south" as fast as it could go. Then the Cowboys pulled off "one of the most dramatic comebacks of the Les Miles era."

Against Missouri in Columbia on Oct. 23, 2004, the OSU offense was simply dreadful for most of the first half against the league's top-rated defense. "Personally, I thought we stunk," declared offensive line coach Chuck Moller. Meanwhile, the Tigers took control of the game with a 17-0 lead. With only 54 seconds left in the half, State had 42 yards total offense; Mizzou had 177.

In that last minute of the half, the offense suddenly clicked. The Cowboys went 80 yards in 50 seconds; quarterback Donovan Woods connected with brother D'Juan Woods for a 12-yard score. Thus had begun the Cowboys' greatest comeback since a 20-point rally for a 21-20 win over Colorado in 1979.

The last half was a complete reversal of the first two quarters. Over the last 31 minutes, OSU rolled up 356 yards while holding the Tigers to 87. Missouri never threatened to score again; State threatened every time it got the ball, missing out on a blocked field goal, two dropped passes in the end zone, and a touchdown called back on a holding penalty.

# COWBOYS

None of those setbacks seemed to dismay the team or slow the offense down. Freshman Jason Ricks kicked a 27-yard field goal in the third quarter to cut the deficit to one score. With 11:36 to play, Woods tied the game at 17 with a 34-yard keeper from the shotgun formation. He followed guard Sam Mayes and tackle Kellen Davis, and left guard Corey Curtis pulled and kicked out the defensive end.

With 55 seconds left to play, Ricks completed the comeback with a 28-yard field goal, the only time in the game OSU was ahead. It was the only time that mattered. 20-17, Cowboys.

Life will have its setbacks whether they result from personal failures or from forces and people beyond your control. Being a Christian and a faithful follower of Jesus Christ doesn't insulate you from getting into deep trouble. Maybe financial problems suffocated you. An illness knocked you down. Or your family was hit with a great tragedy. Life is a series of victories and defeats. Winning isn't about avoiding defeat; it's about getting back up to compete again. It's about making a comeback of your own.

When you avail yourself of God's grace and God's power, your comeback is always greater than your setback. You are never too far behind, and it's never too late in life's game for Jesus to lead you to victory, to turn trouble into triumph. As it was with the Cowboys against Missouri and with the thief on the cross who repented, it's not how you start that counts; it's how you finish.

*I've got faith in my teammates. I knew we were going to get it done.*
*-- Tailback Vernard Morency on the comeback vs. Missouri*

**In life, victory is truly a matter of how you finish
and whether you finish with Jesus at your side.**

# HOMEBODIES

**Read 2 Corinthians 5:1-10.**

*"We . . . would prefer to be away from the body and at home with the Lord" (v. 8).*

**E**ddie Sutton's 1990-91 basketball team was a bunch of home-bodies, unbeatable at home, but they had some extra incentive.

By tying Kansas with a 10-4 Big-Eight record, Sutton's initial team won Oklahoma State's first conference title since 1965 when Henry Iba was coaching. The Cowboys finished the season with a 24-8 record after advancing to the Sweet Sixteen round of the NCAA Tournament before losing.

With the squad described as "an unlikely bunch of players," perhaps the most intriguing player on the team was seven-foot senior center Johnny Pittman. He started all 32 games, averaging eight points and six rebounds per contest. He shot a quite respect-able .518 from the field and held his own well in the pivot. His struggles at the free-throw line, however, became something of a *cause celebre* among the student body.

For the season, he converted a woeful 27 percent of his charity shots. It got so bad that the State students often put their hands together and held them over their heads in an attitude of prayer when Pittman stepped to the line. "I've tried everything," he said after missing six-of-eight free throws in a win over Nebraska. "I don't know what's wrong." He even tried a "one-handed, tilting-to-the-right stance that [made] him resemble a shot-putter."

# COWBOYS

Those same OSU students helped turn Gallagher-Iba Arena "into a frenzied zoo" that winter. The team responded with a spotless 14-0 record at home. The frenetic home crowds weren't all that drove the players, though. As the coach's son, starting point guard Sean Sutton, related, the senior Sutton "told us that if we lost at home, we would have to come in at 5 a.m. the next day and run five miles."

The ultimate homebodies never did have to run.

Home is not necessarily a matter of geography. It may be that place you share with your spouse and your children, whether it's Oklahoma or Alaska. You may feel at home when you return to Stillwater, wondering why you were so eager to leave in the first place. Maybe the home you grew up in still feels like an old shoe, a little worn but comfortable and inviting.

It is no mere happenstance that one of the circumstances of life we most abhor is that of being homeless. That dread results from the sense of home that God has planted in us. Our God is a God of place, and our place is with him.

Thus, we may live a few blocks away from our parents and grandparents or we may relocate every few years, but we will still sometimes feel as though we don't really belong no matter where we are. We don't; our true home is with God in the place Jesus has gone ahead to prepare for us. We are homebodies and we are perpetually homesick.

*I guess we can put our running shoes back on the rack.*
*— Sean Sutton after the 1990-91 Cowboys went 14-0 at home*

**We are continually homesick for our real home, which is with God in Heaven.**

# CONFIDENCE MAN

**Read Micah 7:5-7.**

*"As for me, I will look to the Lord, I will wait for the God of my salvation" (v. 7 NRSV).*

The Cowboys were pretty much getting their brains beat out at halftime, yet they remained confident they would win. Their confidence was not misplaced.

Against Texas A&M on Sept. 24, 2011, the 3-0 Cowboys trailed 20-3 at intermission. "We made mistakes, we had penalties, we missed six or seven tackles, and we looked a little gun shy," said head coach Mike Gundy in explaining the 17-point deficit.

Despite the calamitous situation, the locker room at halftime was calm with both coaches and players relaxed and surprisingly confident. The coaches talked adjustments; the players listened.

Robert Allen, sideline reporter for the Cowboy Radio Network, had his cohorts questioning his sanity when he said at halftime that the game "was not only winnable but . . . was in the bag." Why would he say such a thing? He had seen the team in the locker room. "You just sensed they were fine," he said.

They were. The confident State team established dominance immediately in the last half. Sophomore running back Jeremy Smith led an 80-yard touchdown drive on OSU's first possession. Then safety Daytawion Lowe caused a fumble at midfield and cornerback Justin Gilbert recovered. The Pokes took advantage with Brandon Weeden finding Justin Blackmon in the end zone with an 11-yard toss. Weeden later completed a touchdown pass to Tracy Moore, and when the third quarter ended, State led 24-20. Two fourth-quarter field goals from Quinn Sharp upped the count to 30-20 before A&M scored with 2:20 left. Senior linebacker James Thomas pulled down an interception to kill the Aggies' last hope. On the final play of the game, Blackmon ran out the clock by backtracking 40 yards for an intentional safety.

The confident Cowboys had erased the 20-3 deficit and broken the Aggies' hearts in their own stadium with a 30-29 win.

You need confidence in all areas of your life. You're confident the company you work for will pay you on time, or you wouldn't go to work. You turn the ignition confident your car will start. When you flip a switch, you expect the light to come on.

Confidence in other people and in things is often misplaced, though. Companies go broke; car batteries die; light bulbs burn out. Even the people you love the most sometimes let you down.

So where can you place your trust with absolute confidence you won't be betrayed? In the promises of God.

Such confidence is easy, of course, when everything's going your way, but what about when you cry as Micah did, "What misery is mine!" That's when your confidence in God must be its strongest. That's when you wait for the Lord confident that God will not fail you, that he will never let you down.

*When you have a football team that has won a lot of games and has a lot of confidence, then you can [come from behind].*
*-- Mike Gundy on the win over A&M in 2011*

**People, things, and organizations will let you down; only God can be trusted confidently.**

# BEST FRIENDS

**Read Ecclesiastes 4:9-12.**

*"If one falls down, his friend can help him up. But pity the man who falls and has no one to help him up!" (v. 10)*

**A** friendship that spanned seven decades was reaffirmed before football games with a handshake.

Bob Fenimore is one of the greatest players in Oklahoma State's history. He was the tailback in head coach Jim Lookabaugh's single-wing offense in the mid-1940s when the school was still known as Oklahoma A&M and the team was known as the Aggies. When Fenimore was inducted into the College Football Hall of Fame in 1972, one writer called him "the greatest one-man offense in college football history."

From that tailback position, the "Blond Bomber" ran, passed, and punted the Cowboys to an 8-1 record and a Cotton-Bowl win in 1944 and a 9-0 slate in 1945 that ended with a victory in the Sugar Bowl. As a safety, he intercepted a school-record 18 passes. He was All-America in 1944 and '45, the school's first.

When Fenimore arrived in Stillwater in 1943, he struck up a friendship with another 17-year-old, Neill Armstrong. The right end and defensive end became the program's second All-America in 1946. Fenimore and he lettered four years in both football and track. The friendship lasted until Fenimore's death in 2010.

The bond was so strong that the friendship is memorialized in OSU's Heritage Hall. Inside a display case is a photograph of the two players shaking hands. Armstrong also had the picture hanging up in his office.

The pair always shook hands before each game. In later years Armstrong couldn't remember how the ritual between the friends began. Armstrong kicked off and Fenimore held the ball. "Back in those days," Armstrong recalled, "you didn't set (the football) up on a tee, you just kicked it off the grass so you had to have someone hold it for you and Bob did that." When they got the ball from the officials, they shook hands.

Lend him your car or some money. Provide tea, sympathy, and comfort when she's down. Talk him out of a bad decision like not going to school at State. What wouldn't you do for a good friend?

Like Bob Fenimore and Neill Armstrong, we are all wired for friendship. Our psyche drives us to seek out both the superficial company of others that casual acquaintance provides and the more meaningful intimacy that true friendship furnishes. We are perhaps at our noblest when we selflessly help a friend.

So if we wouldn't think of turning our back on our friends, why would we not be the truest, most faithful friend of all by sharing with them the gospel of Jesus Christ? Without thinking, we give a friend a ride, but we know someone for years and don't do what we can to save her from eternal damnation. Apparently, we are quite willing to spend all of eternity separated from our friends. What kind of lousy friend is that?

*That was just a special friendship you have with a teammate.*
*-- Neill Armstrong on Bob Fenimore*

**A true friend introduces a friend
to his friend Jesus.**

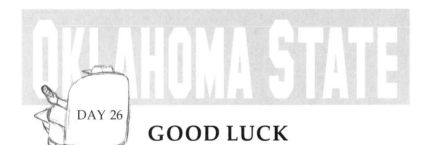

DAY 26

# GOOD LUCK

**Read Acts 1:15-25.**

*"Then they prayed, 'Lord, you know everyone's heart.
Show us which of these two you have chosen.' . . . Then
they cast lots" (vv. 24, 25a).*

**S**ometimes you just have to make your own luck. A Cowboy
defender did just that, and Oklahoma State had a win in the wild-
est shootout the program had ever seen.

On Sept. 22, 2007, Texas Tech rolled up an incredible 718 yards
in offense, the most ever surrendered by the Cowboys. The Red
Raiders scored six touchdowns and a field goal -- and OSU won
the game by four points and a lucky fingernail.

That's because the Pokes rolled to 610 yards and seven touchdowns of their own. For the first time in school history, OSU had
three players who each had more than 100 yards rushing. Tailback
Dantrell Savage had 130 yards, quarterback Zac Robinson had 116
yards, and freshman tailback Kendall Hunter had 113.

In the fourth quarter, Tech held a seven-point lead at 42-35
when receiver Seth Newton took an end-around handoff, pulled
up, and sailed a 33-yard touchdown pass to Jeremy Broadway.
Tech answered with a field goal to lead 45-42. Then with only 1:37
left, tight end Brandon Pettigrew took a short pass over the middle
from Robinson and rumbled 54 yards for a touchdown. 49-45.

But that left way too much time for Tech. On fourth-and-8 from
the OSU 15 with 24 seconds left, Tech took one last shot at the end

zone -- and ran out of luck. The Raider quarterback thought his pass was good for six; his receiver was open.

Cowboy safety Ricky Price did all he could to get there, but he couldn't bat the pass away. All he got on the ball was an apparently harmless fingernail. That little bit of luck was enough, however, to distract the open receiver. The ball bounced off his hands and dropped to the ground. OSU had a wild, luck-aided win.

Ever think sometimes that other people have all the luck? Some guy wins a lottery while you can't get a raise of a few lousy bucks at work. The football takes a lucky bounce the other team's way and State loses a game. If you have any luck to speak of, it's bad.

To ascribe anything that happens in life to blind luck is to believe that random chance controls everything, including you. But here's the truth: Luck exists only as a makeshift explanation for something beyond our ken. Even when the apostles in effect flipped a coin to pick the new guy, they acknowledged that the lots merely revealed to them a decision God had already made.

It's true that we can't explain why some people skate merrily through life while others suffer in horrifying ways. We don't know why good things happen to bad people and vice versa. But none of it results from luck, unless, as the disciples did, you want to attribute that name to the force that does indeed control the universe; you know -- the one more commonly called God.

*I don't think you could say we were lucky to win, but I think we were kind of fortunate not to lose.*
*-- OSU tackle Rodney Harding after a win in 1984*

**A force does exist that is in charge of your life, but it isn't luck; it's God.**

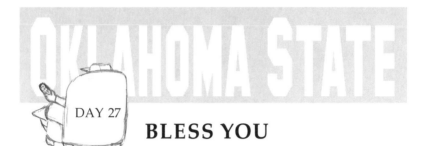

# BLESS YOU

**Read Romans 5:1-11.**

*"We also rejoice in our sufferings because we know that suffering produces perseverance; perseverance, character; and character, hope. And hope does not disappoint us" (vv. 3-5a).*

**T**he Cowboys' season apparently took a turn for the worse when a projected star on defense went down before the first game. The injury turned out to be a blessing for the team.

Defensive coordinator Pat Jones declared that while so-called experts lauded the Miami Hurricane defense of the 1980s with its built-for-speed approach, that style was born in Stillwater in 1983. As much as anything, it came about because of an injury to Jim Krebs. He was a junior college All-American linebacker, who was, according to Jones, "a legit middle linebacker in our 4-3 defense." During two-a-days, Krebs broke an arm and was done.

The scrambling OSU coaches took the approach that "we've got to change our scheme without changing too much." They moved Matt Monger to inside linebacker. A more subtle change involved Warren Thompson, an add-on in the recruiting of junior college running back Joe Miller. He wanted his pal Thompson to come to Stillwater with him and got his wish. The coaches changed Thompson's technique, in fact pretty much eliminating any technique at all. They told him he could now just fire down inside from his defensive end spot. As Jones put it, Thompson "made a million plays for us in this new defense."

To get Thompson on the field the coaches had to move Rodney Harding to defensive tackle. John Washington and All-American Leslie O'Neal completed the front line.

In an effort simply to get the best players on the field in the wake of Krebs' injury, the Cowboy coaches had in effect fostered a new approach to defense: Speed kills! The '83 defense ranked 8th nationally against the rush and ninth in scoring.

A major injury turned out to be a blessing.

We just never know what God is up to. We can know, though, that he's always busy preparing blessings for us and that if we trust and obey him, he will pour out those blessings upon us.

Some of those blessings, however, come disguised as hardship as was the case with the 1983 Cowboys. That's often true in our own lives, too, and it is only after we can look back upon what we have endured that we understand it as a blessing.

The key lies in trusting God, in realizing that God isn't out to destroy us but instead is interested only in doing good for us, even if that means allowing us to endure the consequences of a difficult lesson. God doesn't manage a candy store; more often, he relates to us as a stern but always loving father.

If we truly love and trust God, no matter what our situation is now, he has blessings in store for us. This, above all, is our greatest hope.

*If Krebs doesn't break his arm, does any of this happen? Probably not.*
*-- Pat Jones on the blessings that emerged in 1983 from the injury*

**Life's hardships are often transformed into blessings when we endure them trusting in God.**

# ULTIMATE MAKEOVER

**Read 2 Corinthians 5:11-21.**

*"If anyone is in Christ, he is a new creation; the old has gone, the new has come!" (v. 17)*

The place went berserk on the night the OSU women's basketball program made itself over -- into a contender.

From 1989-1996 under head coach Dick Halterman, the Cowgirls made the NCAA Tournament seven times. The 1990-91 team set a school record for wins with 27, tied for first in the Big 12, and advanced to the Sweet Sixteen.

From 1997-2006, however, wins were hard to come by, and postseason play was just a dream. In 2005-06, the late Kurt Budke's first season, the team went 0-16 in the Big 12.

The turnaround had begun, though. In 2006-07, the team won twenty games, broke even in the conference, and earned a berth in the Big Dance. The question still remained, however: Was that season an aberration or were the Cowgirls back? The question was answered on the night of Jan. 12, 2008.

It was Bedlam. The Sooner women were ranked sixth in the nation. Sophomore Megan Byford realized the night was special long before tipoff as she watched fans pack Gallagher-Iba Arena. When she reported to the scorer's table to enter the game, the place was so loud she couldn't hear. She had no much adrenaline flowing that she had to calm herself down to keep from passing out. "It was just . . . amazing," she said about the atmosphere.

**COWBOYS**

Led by a masterful performance from Andrea Riley, the Cowgirls blasted OU 82-63. Riley scored 45 points with no turnovers. The OSU legend finished up in 2010 as the Big 12's all-time leading scorer. She rewrote the State record book and won the Nancy Lieberman Award in 2010 as the country's best point guard.

The landmark win "changed the program," Byford said. "It kind of made a statement of, 'Hey, we're not the whipping dog of the Big 12 anymore.'"

The win indeed made the program over, re-establishing the Cowgirls as a force to be reckoned with in the Big 12.

Ever considered a makeover? TV shows show us how changes in clothes, hair, and makeup and some weight loss can radically alter the way a person looks. But these changes are only skin deep. Even with a makeover, the real you — the person inside — remains unchanged. How can you make over that part of you?

By giving your heart and soul to Jesus -- just as you give up your hair to the makeover stylist. You won't look any different; you won't dance any better; you won't suddenly start talking smarter. The change is on the inside where you are brand new because the model for all you think and feel is now Jesus. He is the one you care about pleasing. Made over by Jesus, you realize that gaining his good opinion — not the world's — is all that really matters. And he isn't the least interested in how you look but how you act.

*It's one of the greatest moments of my life.*
*-- Andrea Riley on the win over Oklahoma in 2008*

**Jesus is the ultimate makeover artist; he can make you over without changing the way you look.**

# ATTITUDE CHECK

**Read 2 Timothy 1:8-12.**

*"I know whom I have believed, and am convinced that he is able to guard what I have entrusted to him for that day" (v. 12).*

Jack Golden had an interesting attitude about the rigors and grind of two-a-day practices that began the 1999 football season: He was downright glad to be there.

After moving from tight end to linebacker, Golden started ten games for the Cowboys in 1997. He finished fifth on the team in tackles and was looking forward to a good senior season in 1998.

It didn't happen. Instead, Golden wound up in the wrong place at the wrong time. In his case, it was a Stillwater convenience store when he intervened in a fight between a teammate and a stranger. A shotgun showed up, several rounds were fired, and Golden was hit in the right calf. It could have been worse. "I'm very fortunate to still have my life," Golden said.

But it was bad enough. Redshirted in '97, Golden found that sitting helplessly on the sideline watching his teammates play was worse than the shooting. "He was really down and out," said fellow linebacker Tarrell Knauls.

Golden made it through the long season with some help from frequent phone conversations with his mother. He also underwent a change in his attitude about the incident and life in general. "I look at [the shooting] every day and I thank God for it," he said. As a result, he considered football a blessing in a way he had never before. "I come out here to have fun. If things went the other way, I wouldn't have been here."

Golden regained his starting spot in 1999, signed with the New York Giants as a free agent in 2000, and played in two Super Bowls.

Whether life is endured or enjoyed depends largely on our attitudes. We all know pessimists, people whose outlook on life is consistently morose and bleak. We all know optimists, people who in similar circumstances find contentment and happiness. We endure the former; we enjoy the latter. It's only natural.

But there is nothing natural about pessimistic Christians. If anyone on this planet has reason to live in an attitude of unbridled optimism, it's the child of God who has found salvation through Jesus Christ.

Our attitude is a result of our perception of reality, which is as much a reflection of time as anything else: what we have encountered in the past, our present situation, and how we see the future unfolding. People of faith can put their past behind them; all has been forgiven. We can also be buoyed in the present by the realization that all things must pass.

That leaves the greatest source of optimism for the Christian: the certain future that lies ahead. Christ has replaced death with immortality. With our souls entrusted to God through our faith in our Savior, a glorious future with God is ours.

*He's ready to go. He's been flat-out eager all summer.*
*-- OSU head coach Bob Simmons on Jack Golden's attitude in 1999*

**Life with God is good and eternity is better;**
**your attitude should reflect those certainties.**

DAY 30

# KNOW-IT-ALLS

**Read Matthew 13:10-17.**

*"The knowledge of the secrets of the kingdom of heaven has been given to you" (v. 11).*

The Texas A&M Aggies weren't too concerned that they didn't know much about a relatively unknown Cowboy running back. In their case, ignorance certainly wasn't bliss.

Barry Sanders spent his first two seasons in Stillwater (1986-87) as a backup to All-American tailback Thurman Thomas. He was the man, though, in 1988, his Heisman-Trophy winning season.

"We had a good team. We had a very good defense," said Aggie head coach Jackie Sherrill about his 1988 squad. OSU head coach Pat Jones echoed that assessment, declaring, "They had great players." The player they didn't have, though, was Sanders.

The teams met in Stillwater on Sept. 24 in the second game of the season. It took 72 seconds for Sherrill and his Aggies to learn who Sanders was. On third and long, the Pokes ran a routine draw play. "He took the ball and we looked like we had it defended pretty well," Sherrill recalled. "We didn't even touch him."

He went 58 yards; the Aggies never recovered. They fumbled, and OSU scored and added a quick field goal for a 17-0 lead. It was 38-7 at halftime. Sanders was done for the day after three quarters as the Cowboys romped to a 52-15 win.

By the standards Sanders established that remarkable season, the A&M game wasn't really anything special. He had 157 yards on 20 carries (nearly 8 yards a lug) and scored three touchdowns, including a 61-yard punt return.

But Sherrill, who had no idea what was coming, knew he had seen something special as he never expected to see his defense dominated the way Sanders did that day. "To see the way he ran through us was pretty amazing," he said.

Like teams preparing for a game, we can never know too much. We once thought our formal education ended when we entered the workplace, but now we have constant training sessions, conferences, and seminars to keep us current whether our expertise is in auto mechanics or medicine. Many areas require graduate degrees now as we scramble to stay abreast of new discoveries and information. And still we never know it all.

Nowhere, though is the paucity of our knowledge more stark than it is when we consider God. We will never know even a fraction of all there is to apprehend about the creator of the universe – with one important exception. God has revealed all we need to know about the kingdom of heaven to ensure our salvation. He has opened to us great and eternal secrets.

All we need to know about getting into Heaven is right there in the Bible. With God, ignorance is no excuse and knowledge is salvation.

*I really didn't know much about Barry Sanders, but I knew more than I wanted to by the end of that game.*
-- *Jackie Sherrill after the '88 OSU game*

**When it comes to our salvation, we can indeed know it all because God has revealed to us everything we need to know.**

# GOAL ORIENTED

**Read 1 Peter 1:3-12.**

*"For you are receiving the goal of your faith, the salvation of your souls" (v. 9).*

Before the 2002 football season started, junior tailback Tatum Bell set a goal for himself. As the season wound down, it looked as though that goal would elude him. And then he did something spectacular.

Bell's goal was to rush for 1,000 yards. He ended the regular season with 936, but the Cowboys' 7-5 record that included wins over Nebraska and Oklahoma earned them a berth in the Houston Bowl against Southern Mississippi. So he had another shot at his goal.

But Bell and the OSU offense ran into a defense specifically set up to shut down the running game, and it did a good job of it. After three quarters, Bell had a grand total of 22 yards. "As the game was going along, I was like, 'Aw, I'm not going to get my 1,000,'" Bell said. But he wasn't just worried about his 1,000 yards; after jumping out to an early 10-0 lead, OSU trailed 23-20 heading into the final fifteen minutes.

Luke Phillips tied the score with his third field goal. Then on the next OSU possession, Bell followed a block from senior fullback Mike Denard on a counter up the middle and scored from 22 yards out. He didn't have his 1,000 yards yet, but he had given the Cowboys a 30-23 lead with 8:07 left in the game.

Bell wasn't finished. When senior linebacker Greg Richmond pressured the Southern Miss quarterback into an incompletion on third down, the Cowboys got the ball back. That was the good news; the bad news was that a 51-yard punt died on the State 2.

On the same play as the touchdown run, Bell burst across the line of scrimmage untouched, moved to the outside, and sped 88 yards. He had his 1,000 yards and when Phillips kicked his fourth field goal with 5:15 left, the Cowboys had a win. 33-23.

Bell finished the season with 1, 096 yards, his goal achieved.

What are your goals for your life? Have you ever thought them out? Or do you just shuffle along living for your paycheck and whatever fun you can seek out instead of pursuing some greater purpose?

Now try this one: What is the goal of your faith life? You go to church to worship God. You read the Bible and study God's word to learn about God and how God wants you to live. But what is it you hope to achieve? What is all that stuff about? For what purpose do you believe that Jesus Christ is God's son?

The answer is actually quite simple: The goal of your faith life is your salvation, and this is the only goal in life that matters. Nothing you will ever seek is as important or as eternal as getting into Heaven and making sure that everybody you know and love will be there too one day.

*I wanted to be the leading rusher on the team and be a 1,000-yard back.*
*-- Tatum Bell on his goals for the 2002 season*

**The most important goal of your life**
**is to get to Heaven and to help as many people**
**as you can to get there one day too.**

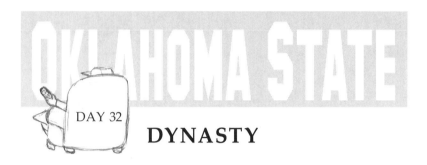

# DYNASTY

**Read 2 Samuel 7:8-17.**

*"Your house and your kingdom will endure forever before me; your throne will be established forever" (v. 16).*

Only one word succinctly and correctly describes the wrestling program at Oklahoma State: dynasty.

Since its inception during the 1914-15 school year and through the 2012-13 season, the Cowboy wrestlers have won 34 national titles, the most of any sport at any major school. Southern Cal is a distant second with its 26 titles in men's outdoor track. The program has also won 47 conference titles, including the 2013 Big 12 championship.

It's difficult to believe but the program went winless its first two seasons. Of course, they had only one meet per season. That second season, though, saw the arrival of Ed Gallagher (See Devotion No. 56.), and the dynasty began. The NCAA sponsored its first national tournament in 1928, and the Cowboys won it -- and the next three titles and nine of the next eleven. From the 1919-20 season through the 1930-31 season, the Cowboys never lost a dual meet, grappling to 70 straight wins.

The true test of a dynasty is whether it can survive the loss of the coach who created it. Gallagher died on Aug. 28, 1940, a week shy of his 54th birthday. The torch was passed to Art Griffith, a high school wrestling coach. The dynasty lived on. Griffith's teams won eight national titles in his thirteen seasons. After him came Myron Roderick, one of his wrestlers, who won seven titles. The dynasty suffered a hiccup with no national titles from 1971-1989. Then along came John Smith who "re-established the dominance of OSU over the rest of the wrestling world." The Cowboys won four straight national crowns from 2003-06.

As powerful and established as it is, the dynasty that is OSU wrestling doesn't win every title. History teaches us that kingdoms, empires, countries, and even sports programs rise and fall. Dynasties end as events and circumstances conspire and align to snap all winning streaks.

Your life is like that; you win some and lose some. You get a promotion on Monday and your son gets arrested on Friday. You breeze through your annual physical but your dog dies. You finally line up a date with that cutie next door and get sent out of town on business.

Only one dynasty will never end because it is based upon an everlasting promise from God. God promised David the king an enduring line in the appearance of one who would establish God's kingdom forever. That one is Jesus Christ, the reigning king of God's eternal and unending dynasty.

The only way to lose out on that one is to stand on the sidelines and not get in the game.

*No other school has a tradition in any sport as strong as the dynasty Oklahoma State has established in wrestling.*
*-- from 'Cowboy Wrestling: Dynasty Defined' at okstate.com*

**All dynasties and win streaks end except the one**
**God established with Jesus as its king;**
**this one never loses and never will.**

DAY 33

# A SURE THING

**Read Romans 8:28-30.**

*"We know that in all things God works for the good of those who love him, who have been called according to his purpose" (v. 28).*

**R**ichetti Jones told the Fiesta Bowl people to go ahead and pass out the winners' hats and shirts. After all, an Oklahoma State win was a sure thing.

On Jan. 2, 2012, Oklahoma State and Stanford got together and put on one of the most exciting bowl games in history. With 1:51 left to play, All-Big 12 running back Joseph Randle capped a 67-yard drive with a 4-yard touchdown run. The extra point tied the game at 38, and that's the way it stayed. Overtime.

On its possession, Stanford missed a field goal. Then on the Cowboys' second play, senior wide receiver and former walk-on Colton Chelf made a fingertip catch of a pass from Brandon Weeden, was hit by a Cardinal, and dived for the end zone. The arms went up to signal a touchdown and the celebration began.

A review, though, determined that Chelf's knee had touched turf a half-yard short of the goal line. The unperturbed Cowboys set about winning their first BCS bowl game a second time and establishing a school record with their twelfth win of the season. On the first play, Weeden took the snap, dashed to the center of the field, and took a knee.

That meant the game was turned over to All-American kicker

Quinn Sharp. Stanford called a time out. On the sideline, defensive end Jones noticed some Fiesta Bowl officials standing by with boxes of hats and shirts for the winners. "I told them just pass those out because Quinn is going to make this kick," he said.

He did. Connor Sinko snapped the ball, Wes Harlan held it, and Sharp drilled it through the uprights. 41-38 Cowboys.

Football games aren't played on paper. That is, the outcome isn't a sure thing. You attend an Oklahoma State game expecting the Cowboys to win, but you don't know for sure. If you did, why bother to go? Any football game worth watching carries with it an element of uncertainty.

Life doesn't get played on paper either, which means that living, too, comes bearing uncertainty. You never know what's going to happen tomorrow or even an hour from now. Oh, sure, you think you know. Right now you may be certain that you'll be at work Monday morning, that you'll have a job next month, and that you'll be happily and comfortably married to the same spouse five years from now. Life's uncertainties, though, can intervene at any time and disrupt those sure things you count on.

Ironically, while you can't know for sure about this afternoon, you can know for certain about forever. Eternity is a sure thing because it's in God's hands. Your unwavering faith and God's sure promises lock in a certain future for you.

*I was thinking, 'Quinn, hurry up and make this kick so I can get my hat and shirt.'*
*-- Richetti Jones on the winning field goal in the Fiesta Bowl*

**Life is unpredictable and tomorrow is uncertain;**
**only eternity with or without God is a sure thing.**

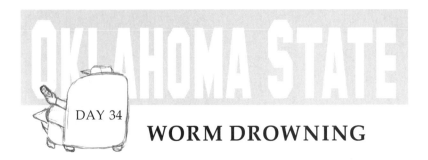

DAY 34

# WORM DROWNING

**Read Mark 1:16-20.**

*"'Come, follow me,' Jesus said, 'and I will make you
fishers of men'" (v. 17).*

**W**hen Rashaun Woods visited Stillwater as a high-school recruit, he found what he was looking for: a country setting and
some good fishing holes.

From 2000-03, Woods set Big-12 records at Oklahoma State
with 293 receptions for 4,414 yards and 42 touchdowns. He was
a two-time All-America and OSU's first-ever All-Big 12 wideout.
His seven touchdown receptions against SMU in 2003 was an
NCAA record.

Footballs weren't all that Woods could catch. During his collegiate days, he harbored dreams of eventually making a living as
a pro bass fisherman. "It's a dream I have," he said. "It's for real."

Woods said he chose to play football for Oklahoma State in part
because of the country setting that made fishing readily available
for him. Not surprisingly, he didn't get much fishing done during
football season, but he carried a fishing pole in his car all the time
just in case the opportunity came along.

Woods and his five siblings grew up on ten acres in the country.
His granddad taught him to play football; his dad taught him to
fish, letting him drown his first worm before the was 3 years old.

Woods really got hooked on fishing, though, in high school. He
stopped by an uncle's pond and, according to Woods, reeled in

forty or fifty bass weighing at least two pounds each in less than two hours. That did it.

Woods' dad, Larry, conceded that his son has a gift for pulling them in. "Usually when we go, he ends up catching the most and the biggest," Larry said. "People tease him and tell him he can catch fish out of the toilet," Rashaun's mother, Juana, said.

The worst fishing trip you ever had may have included numbing cold, nary a nibble, a flat tire, or any combination of misadventures. You dragged in late, knowing full well you had to get up early next morning. Still, as Rashaun Woods would tell you, it was better than a good day at work, wasn't it?

What if somebody in authority looked you square in the eyes and told you, "Go Fish"? How quickly would you trip over anybody who got in your way? Well, Jesus did exactly that, commanding his followers to fish for people who are drowning and lost without him.

Jesus issued that command with the utmost seriousness. For the men of his time, fishing was neither for pleasure nor for sport. Rather, it was hard work, a demanding, hardscrabble way to support a family.

Fishing for men and women for Jesus is likewise hard work, but it is such the essence of the Christian mission that a fish has become the symbol of the faith itself.

*He would rather fish than eat.*

*-- Juana Woods on her son, Rashaun*

**Jesus understood the passion people have for fishing and commanded that it become not just a hobby but a way of life.**

# SMART MOVE

### Read 1 Kings 4:29-34; 11:1-6.

*"[Solomon] was wiser than any other man. . . . As Solomon grew old, his wives turned his heart after other gods, and his heart was not fully devoted to the Lord his God" (vv. 4:31, 11:4).*

Cowboy head coach Jimmy Johnson made a smart move in the fall of 1982: He moved Ernest Anderson from fullback to tailback.

Not too much was expected of Anderson when he arrived in Stillwater in 1979. At 5'8" inches and 165 lbs, he was a relatively scrawny running back who in high school had never rushed for 1,000 yards in a season or 200 yards in a game. The coaches figured, though, he could become a pretty good player if they could beef him up. Anderson had never lifted weights; it was time.

It was not time, however, for success on the football field. In his first collegiate game, Anderson bruised a knee ligament so badly that he missed the entire '79 season. "That freshman year was tough," Anderson later admitted. "I had my bags packed on several occasions."

But with encouragement from his family and his coaches, he stayed. All the while, he was in a weight room, so dedicated that during the summer of '82, he lifted weights three hours each day after working construction for nine hours beside his father.

Then before the 1982 season began, Johnson made his smart move; he shifted this unknown running back to tailback in the

Cowboys' power-I formation. His first two seasons Anderson had 232 rushes; in 1982 alone, he had 353.

The results were dramatic and historic. On the Pokes' first play from scrimmage in '82, Anderson busted a 74-yard touchdown run. He ran for 220 yards that game. He went on to lead the nation in rushing with 1,877 yards and was All-America.

Smart move, coach. Very smart move.

Remember that time you wrecked the car when you spilled hot coffee on your lap? That cold morning you fell out of the boat? The time you gave your honey a tool box for her birthday?

Formal education notwithstanding, we all make some dumb moves sometimes because time spent in a classroom is not an accurate gauge of common sense. Folks impressed with their own smarts often grace us with erudite pronouncements that we intuitively recognize as flawed, unworkable, or simply wrong.

A good example is the observation that great intelligence and scholarship are inherently incompatible with a deep and abiding faith in God. That is, the more we know, the less we believe. Any incompatibility occurs, however, only because we begin to trust in our own wisdom rather than the wisdom of God. We forget, as Solomon did, that God is the ultimate source of all our knowledge and wisdom and that even our ability to learn is a gift from God.

Not smart at all.

*We knew last year [1981] that Ernest [Anderson] was our best runner. [H]e was also our best fullback, and we needed him there to block.*
*-- OSU running backs coach Frank Falks*

**Being truly smart means trusting in God's wisdom rather than only in our own knowledge.**

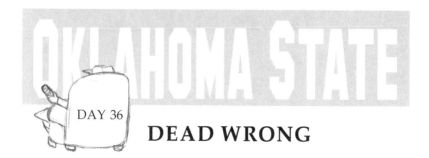

DAY 36

# DEAD WRONG

### Read Matthew 26:14-16; 27:1-10.

*"When Judas, who had betrayed him, saw that Jesus was condemned, he was seized with remorse" (v. 27:3).*

The doctors told Desmond Mason's parents that their toddler would probably never walk again and would certainly never run again. They were wrong.

As a senior forward in 1999-2000, Mason was the leading scorer for a Cowboy team that went 27-7 and advanced to the Elite Eight in the NCAA Tournament. *Sports Illustrated* said of Mason that he went on Cowboy road trips "looking like a struggling Manhattan artist on his way to a Soho gallery." That's because the studio art major always lugged around some of his works-in-progress. The only exception to Mason's traveling studio was his sculpture. "You know, blowtorches and all," he said.

That Mason would tinker with a blowtorch is unlikely considering what happened when he was 3. On a blazing Texas summer day in 1981, he was asleep in the front seat of his dad's parked car when a friend pulled up with his car's radiator hissing. He popped the hood and unscrewed the cap without releasing the pressure. Boiling radiator fluid sprayed through the adjacent car, right onto the sleeping toddler's chest, back, and legs.

"He was smoking," said Desmond's dad, Johnney. "I snatched him out through the car window, and the steam was so hot coming off his clothes that I couldn't even hold on to him." Dad pulled

Desmond's jeans off, and skin came with the pants.

The doctors made an initial prognosis that the toddler would be fortunate to ever walk again and would assuredly never be able to run. He spent three months in the hospital, a year in physical therapy, and then another year wearing a cast to straighten out a leg left crooked by the skin grafts.

When he was 7, though, Desmond started playing basketball and football with no ill effects at all. He proved the doctors wrong right on through four OSU seasons and ten NBA years.

There's wrong, there's dead wrong, and there's Judas wrong. We've all been wrong in our lives, but we can at least honestly ease our conscience by telling ourselves we'll never be as wrong as Judas was. A close examination of Judas' actions, however, reveals that we can indeed replicate in our own lives the mistake Judas made that drove him to suicidal despair.

Judas ultimately regretted his betrayal of our Lord, but his sorrow and remorse, however boundless, could not save him. His attempt to undo his initial wrong was futile because he tried to fix everything himself rather than turning to God in repentance and begging for mercy.

While we can't literally betray Jesus to his enemies as Judas did, we can match Judas' failure in our own lives by not turning to God in Jesus' name and asking for forgiveness for our sins. In that case, we ultimately will be as dead wrong as Judas was.

*Desmond [Mason] does things humans aren't supposed to do.*
*-- OSU's Doug Gottlieb as his teammate proved the doctors wrong*

**A sin is the first wrong; failing to ask God
for forgiveness of it is the second.**

# LESSON LEARNED

**Read Psalm 143.**

*"Teach me to do your will, for you are my God" (v. 10).*

The Cowboys used a hard, bitter lesson they had learned during the season to pull out a bowl-game win.

With the fourth quarter ticking away in the 2006 Independence Bowl, State was sitting comfortably ahead of Alabama 31-17. Then suddenly it all went wrong. Alabama returned a punt 86 yards for a touchdown, and OSU fumbled the kickoff. The Tide capitalized. In the horrifying span of two minutes and nine seconds, the 14-point Cowboy lead had become a 31-31 tie with only 3:18 left on the clock.

The Cowboys had seen it before. Four times during the season -- one described as "alternating brilliance with misery" -- they had lost games that had come down to the final play. Thus, they entered the bowl with a 6-6 record  convinced they the best six-loss team in the country.

So here they were with yet another chance to suffer some more fourth-quarter heartbreak. "I just thought we were right back where we had been all year," quarterback Bobby Reid said.

Not quite. This time the team showed it had learned a lesson from all those close losses. "Nobody was panicking," Reid said. "I told the guys it was time for us to finish. Our seniors took care of it. We did what we had to do."

Indeed they did. The Cowboys answered the sudden Alabama

blitz by maintaining their composure. They went 74 yards chiefly behind a dazzling series from junior tailback Dantrell Savage. He started the drive with a 23-yard romp.

Seven plays later, on third-and-9, Savage turned a Reid screen pass into a 26-yard gain to the Alabama 15. With eight seconds left, Jason Ricks booted a 27-yard field goal.

Lesson learned. Game won 34-31.

Learning about anything in life requires a combination of education and experience. Education is the accumulation of facts that we call knowledge; experience is the acquisition of wisdom and discernment, which add purpose and understanding to our knowledge. Education without experience just doesn't have much practical value in our world today.

The most difficult way to learn is trial and error; just dive in blindly and mess up all over the place. The best way to learn is through example coupled with a set of instructions. Someone has gone ahead to show you the way and has written down all the information you need to follow.

In teaching us the way to live godly lives, God chose the latter method. He set down in his book the habits, actions, and attitudes that make for a way of life in accordance with his wishes. He also sent us Jesus to explain and to illustrate.

God teaches us not only how to exist but how to live. We just need to be attentive students.

*It is evident [we] learned how to win and how to overcome adversity.*
*— Mike Gundy after the 2006 Independence Bowl*

**To learn from Jesus is to learn what life is all about and how God means for us to live it.**

# GIVEN THE BOOT

### Read Genesis 37:1-11.

*"Israel loved Joseph more than all his children, because he was the son of his old age: and he made him a coat of many colours" (v. 3 KJV).*

For a while, a disconcerted Pat Jones thought he would have to pony up $3,000 for a pair of boots he probably would never wear.

The Cowboys of 1987 went 9-2 and headed off to El Paso for the Sun Bowl on Christmas Day. As Jones, the Cowboy head coach put it, "The Sun Bowl people did a great job making sure we had a good time." They even assigned one person to escort the head coaches around.

Jones' escort took him one day to the shop of a manufacturer of custom-made boots. The people there told him to pick out whatever he wanted for his own pair. "I didn't really wear or know anything about boots," Jones recalled, "but they let me pick out the style, toe, heel, and everything else."

The head Cowboy picked out what he called "some beautiful tan-looking stuff -- a kind of lizard skin or reptile or something." They measured his foot and told him they would put "the OSU brand, my initials, and the whole shebang on them." Jones asked how much the boots would cost if they weren't complimentary, and he was told about $3,000.

Back at practice that day, Jones bragged to his assistant coaches about his beautiful custom-made boots, making sure they knew he was getting a $3,000 pair for free. "A lot of these guys were boot guys, so they were all impressed," Jones said.

But then running backs coach Bill Shimek spoke up. He had been to the Sun Bowl several years before as an assistant at Oklahoma. He said, "They let Barry Switzer do the same thing, . . . but two months later he got the boots with a bill in the box."

Jones spent the whole practice worrying about paying for those $3,000 boots before Shimek fessed up to his tall tale.

Contemporary society proclaims that it's all about the clothes. Buy that new suit or dress and all the sparkling accessories -- maybe even those fancy boots -- and you'll be a brand new person. The changes are only cosmetic, though; under those clothes, you're the same person. Consider Joseph, for instance, prancing about in his pretty new clothes; he was still a spoiled little tattletale whom his brothers detested enough to sell into slavery.

Jesus never taught that we should run around half-naked or wear only second-hand clothes from the local mission. He did warn us, though, against making consumer items such as clothes a priority in our lives. A follower of Christ seeks to emulate Jesus not through material, superficial means such as wearing special clothing like a robe and sandals. Rather, the disciple desires to match Jesus' inner beauty and serenity -- whether the clothes the Christian wears are the sables of a king or the rags of a pauper.

*I went through the whole practice thinking that they were going to send me a bill for those boots.*

-- Pat Jones at the '87 Sun Bowl

**Where Jesus is concerned,
clothes don't make the person; faith does.**

DAY 39

# MYSTERIOUS WAYS

**Read Romans 11:25-36.**

*"O the depth of the riches and wisdom and knowledge of God! How unsearchable are his judgments and how inscrutable his ways!" (v. 33 NRSV)*

Justin Blackmon overnight found himself facing life in a place that was one big mystery. He didn't like it either.

Blackmon was 8 years old and quite happily ensconced in the Southern California lifestyle. In fact, he had just returned from a week of swimming, hiking, and tubing at a church camp when his father changed his world forever. Dad had taken a new job that required the family move to some unknown place called Ardmore, Okla. "The entire state was a total mystery," Blackmon later recalled about his initial reaction. He said that dread set in; he didn't even know where Oklahoma was.

Ardmore certainly presented a culture shock for the family, particularly the boys. However, by the time "sightings of turtles and deer crossing the local streets became normal," young Justin was thriving in this strange new world. Football, basketball, track, even ice hockey -- he excelled in them all, giving up baseball to concentrate on track. He sang in an award-winning choir. During his first two years of high school football, he stripped off his shoulder pads at halftime to drum with the marching band.

When he left Ardmore, he relocated, of course, to Stillwater, and the rest is Cowboy football legend.

# COWBOYS

On April 23, 2011, that once-mysterious town celebrated Justin Blackmon Day. He returned home a hero, greeted by hundreds of friends and supporters. Children lined up for his autograph. Someone proposed that a street be named for him. "It was a homecoming the likes of which Blackmon never dreamed of, in a place he once couldn't find on a map."

The good Lord sure works in mysterious ways. It's an old saying among people of faith, an acknowledgment of the limits of our understanding of God. It's true, which serves to make God even more tantalizing because human nature loves a good mystery. We relish the challenge of uncovering what somebody else wants to hide. We are intrigued by a perplexing whodunit, a rousing round of Clue, or TV shows such as *NCIS*.

Unlike Justin Blackmon and Ardmore, some mysteries are just beyond our knowing. Events in our lives that are in actuality the mysterious ways of God remain so to us because we can't see the divine machinations. We can see only the results, appreciate that God was behind it all, and give him thanks and praise.

God has revealed much about himself, especially through Jesus, but still much remains unknowable. Why does he tolerate the existence of evil? What does he really look like? Why is he so fond of bugs? We don't know, and for now we can't know.

We can know for sure, though, that God is love, and so we proceed with life, assured that one day all mysteries will be revealed.

*Things would be a lot different if we didn't move. I'm glad we did.*
*– Justin Blackmon on no-longer-mysterious Ardmore*

**God keeps much about himself shrouded in
mystery, but one day we will see and understand.**

DAY 40

# IMPRESSIONS

**Read Mark 6:1-6.**

*"And [Jesus] was amazed at their lack of faith" (v. 6).*

Eric Guerrero wanted to impress a wrestling legend -- and he lost. What happened after he lost made the lasting impression.

Guerrero is an Oklahoma State and college wrestling legend. From 1996-99, he won the NCAA individual championship three times and was a four-time All-America. In his senior season, he recorded a 31-0 record. He joined the staff of fellow legend John Smith at OSU in 2000 and was promoted to head assistant coach in 2009.

Guerrero's dad wrestled in high school, and the son "was not out of diapers before his father began teaching him the art of the takedown." As mom recalled, when Eric was in high school, the pair would "just move the coffee table and go at it on the living room floor."

When Guerrero was 12, he first met Smith at a U.S. Open meet. Guerrero saw in Smith a mentor who, when he wrestled, worked his brain as hard as he did in muscles. "I shook his hand and got him to sign my hat," Guerrero recalled. "Then I wanted him to see me wrestle."

That didn't happen until four years later at a national meet in North Dakota. With Smith looking on, Guerrero got beat, thus failing to make the impression he wanted to. Or so he thought.

It didn't turn out that way at all. Smith was impressed with the way Guerreo handled the defeat. "What I really enjoyed was the frustration [Guerreo] showed after the match," Smith said. "You could tell it truly hurt him. I like to see pain after a loss, instead of somebody saying, 'No big deal, tomorrow's another day.'"

Smith was impressed enough to offer Guerrero a scholarship, and the rest is Oklahoma State history.

You bought that canary convertible mainly to impress the girls; a white Accord would transport you more efficiently. You seek out subtle but effective ways to gain the boss' approval. You may be all grown up now, but you still want your parents' favor. You dress professionally but strikingly and take your prospective clients to that overpriced steak house.

In our lives we are constantly seeking to impress someone else so they'll remember us and respond favorably to us. That's exactly the impression we should be making upon Jesus because in God's scheme for salvation, only the good opinion of Jesus Christ matters. On the day when we stand before God, our fate for eternity rests upon Jesus remembering and responding favorably to us.

We don't want to be like the folks in Jesus' hometown. Oh, they impressed him all right: with their lack of faith in him. This is not the impression we want to make on our Lord and Savior.

*You can't just beat a team. You have to leave a lasting impression in their minds so they never want to see you again.*
*-- Soccer legend Mia Hamm*

**Jesus is the only one worth impressing,**
**and it is the depth of your faith –**
**or the lack of it – that impresses him.**

# FAITHFUL LIVES

**Read Hebrews 11:1-12.**

*"Faith is the substance of things hoped for, the evidence of things not seen" (v. 1 NKJV).*

Artrell Woods was grateful for what his doctors did for him, but he knew that the real power behind his comeback from an awful accident was God.

A sophomore, Woods was expected to start in 2007 at wide receiver opposite Adarius Bowman. Only a week after starring in the '07 spring game, however, Woods was injured during a routine workout with the weights. His ankle rolled over as he walked to return a weight to the rack, and he fell, bearing that weight. He suffered a dislocated vertebra; as he lay on the floor, he realized he was paralyzed since he couldn't feel his legs.

Immediate surgery repaired the damage to Woods' spine, but doctors remained unsure whether he would ever walk normally again. Woods, on the other hand, boldly and confidently predicted he would play football for the Cowboys again. "I had faith," he explained. "I prayed on it every night, and I gave God the glory."

He had his faith in the right place. Within three weeks, the progress he had made was dubbed "nothing short of a miracle."

Woods admitted, though, that it wasn't always easy. "I've had some days where I was real angry with everybody, and thinking about my season," he said. But he kept the faith and found himself especially buoyed when his teammates visited him.

# COWBOYS

When the 2007 season began, Woods was in a full-torso brace. When the 2008 season began, he was on the field with the special teams units and a backup to DeMarcus Conner at one wideout position. "It's a pretty amazing story," said Cowboy head coach Mike Gundy.

In the November 1 rout of Iowa State, Woods caught a 7-yard pass. The crowd gave him a standing ovation with coaches and teammates joining in the applause.

As it does for Artrell Woods, your faith forms the heart and soul of who you are. Faith in people, things, ideologies, and concepts to a large extent determines how you spend your life. You believe in the Cowboys, in your family, in the basic goodness of Americans, in freedom and liberty, and in abiding by the law. These beliefs mold you and make you the person you are.

This is all great stuff, of course, that makes for decent human beings and productive lives. None of it, however, is as important as what you believe about Jesus. To have faith in Jesus is to believe his message of hope and salvation as recorded in the Bible. True faith in Jesus, however, has an additional component; it must also include a personal commitment to him. In other words, you don't just believe in Jesus; you live for him.

Faith in Jesus does more than shape your life; it determines your eternity.

*I knew [God] was going to get me to this point, sooner or later.*
*-- Artrell Woods before the 2008 season opener, in which he played*

**Your belief system is the foundation upon which**
**you build your earthly life; faith in Jesus**
**is the foundation for your eternal life.**

# MAKE NO MISTAKE

**Read Mark 14:66-72.**

*"Then Peter remembered the word Jesus had spoken to him: 'Before the rooster crows twice you will disown me three times.' And he broke down and wept" (v. 72).*

**C**olorado made a mistake, and the Cowboys pounced on it to score a late touchdown and pull out a win.

When the Buffaloes and the Cowboys got together at Lewis Field on Oct. 11, 1997, the clash between the two symbols of the Old West was a battle of ranked teams. At 6-0 for only the second time in school history, Oklahoma State was ranked 20th while Colorado came in at No. 24 in the polls.

OSU's big weapon in the game was sophomore kicker Tim Sydnes, who knocked home four field goals. Redshirt freshman quarterback Tony Lindsay did his part, throwing the game-winning touchdown and rushing for 126 yards and another score.

State led 19-14 at halftime thanks to an interception and 40-yard touchdown return from senior cornerback Kevin Williams. Only the first of Colorado's two backbreaking mistakes kept the Buffs out of the end zone as the first half ended. With the ball at the OSU 22 and time running out, a Colorado receiver hauled in a 10-yard pass but failed to get out of bounds before he was tackled. Colorado didn't have time to run another play.

State took a 26-22 lead with 11:21 left when Lindsay got in from 1 yard out. Colorado answered with a score to lead 29-26 and then seemed to have the game in hand when OSU made a mistake of its own, fumbling at the Buffalo 7 with only 3:45 on the clock.

But with 2:45 to play, Colorado made the game's biggest mistake. From their 23, the Buffs tried a pass, and Maurice Simpson intercepted it. Two plays later, Lindsay found tight end Alonzo Mayes for a 19-yard touchdown pass with only 1:56 on the clock.

Thanks to a big mistake, OSU had a 33-29 win.

It's distressing but it's true: Like football teams and Simon Peter, we all make mistakes. Only one perfect man ever walked on this earth, and no one of us is he. Some mistakes are just dumb. Like locking yourself out of your car or falling into a swimming pool with your clothes on.

Other mistakes are more significant and carry with them the potential for devastation. Like heading down a path to addiction. Committing a crime. Walking out on a spouse and the children.

All these mistakes, however, from the momentarily annoying to the life-altering tragic, share one aspect: They can all be forgiven in Christ. Other folks may not forgive us; we may not even forgive ourselves. But God will forgive us when we call upon him in Jesus' name.

Thus, the twofold fatal mistake we can make is ignoring the fact that we will die one day and subsequently ignoring the fact that Jesus is the only way to shun Hell and enter Heaven. We absolutely must get this one right.

*If you're not making mistakes, you're not doing anything.*
-- *John Wooden*

**Only one mistake we make sends us to Hell
when we die: ignoring Jesus while we live.**

# THE BIG TIME

### Read Revelation 21:22-27; 22:1-6.

*"They will see his face, and his name will be on their foreheads. . . . And they will reign for ever and ever" (vv. 22:4, 5c).*

**U**ndefeated season. Top 10 ranking. Big 12 championship. BCS bowl. It doesn't get any more big time than that. What the Cowboys needed was a pair of big-time plays to keep it all alive.

The OSU-Kansas State game of Nov. 5, 2011, was such a big-time contest that *ESPN on ABC* rolled into Stillwater with Brent Musburger and Kirk Herbstreit in tow. In the locker room before the game, Mike Gundy talked about how high the stakes were against the Wildcats, who would go on to win ten games.

Ultimately, the outcome of the game depended on which team could make big plays in the last minute. It was the Cowboys.

The game was tied at 45 with 3:18 left to play. In a big-time drive, Brandon Weeden took the offense 65 yards in four plays with Joseph Randle breaking off a 23-yard run for the touchdown. The problem was that the drive took only 1:02 off the clock. Had the Cowboys given K-State too much time?

They had. The Wildcats raced downfield until they faced a second and goal at the OSU 5 with only five ticks on the clock. A "little" man then made a big play. Cornerback Brodrick Brown used every inch of his 5'8" body and perfect timing to leap up, stretch out, and bat away an end-zone pass. Kansas State had one second left and thus another play.

Once again, someone had to step up big-time for the Cowboys. Senior defensive end Richetti Jones, who led the team in prayer when they arrived at the stadium, was the man. He rushed hard and closed on the Cat quarterback before his receivers came open. His desperate pass fell harmlessly to the end-zone turf.

The big-time Cowboys had a 52-45 win.

We often look around at our current situation and dream of hitting the big time. We might look longingly at that vice-president's office or daydream about the day when we're the boss, maybe even of our own business. We may scheme about ways to make a lot of money, or at least more than we're making now. We may even consciously seek out fame and power.

Making it big is just part of the American dream. It's the heart of that which drives immigrants to leave everything they know and come to this country.

The truth, though, is that all of this so-called "big-time" stuff we so earnestly cherish is actually only small potatoes. If we want to speak of the real big-time, we better think about God and his dwelling place in Heaven. There we not only see God and Jesus face to face, but we reign. God puts us in charge.

It just doesn't get any bigger than that – and it's ours for the taking. Or at least for the believing.

*When [OSU] fans in the future think about the 2011 season, . . . this is the play that is going to come up often as being instrumental.*
-- More Than a Championship *on Brodrick Brown's big-time play*

**Living with God, hanging out with Jesus,
and reigning in Heaven – now that's big time.**

# JUGGERNAUT

**Read Revelation 20.**

*"Fire came down from heaven and devoured them. And the devil, who deceived them, was thrown into the lake of burning sulfur, where the beast and the false prophet had been thrown" (vv. 9b-10a).*

The golf national title was generally considered to belong to the juggernaut that was Wake Forest. Except that the Deacons ran into a juggernaut from Stillwater.

When the teams gathered in Albuquerque for the 1976 NCAA golf championship, the tournament field was Wake Forest and everyone else. The Demon Deacons had won eleven straight titles by an average of 24 strokes and showed up in New Mexico with pretty much the same guys who had won the past two titles. They had won the '75 championship by a staggering 33 strokes.

Thus, most folks were searching for a way to stop the juggernaut that was Wake Forest. Not everyone, however, was willing to hand the tournament trophy over to Wake in advance. OSU coach Mike Holder was one of those.

The Cowboys had started out well but had faded late in the 1975 tournament. This time around, though, Holder felt he had a team that could hang with Wake Forest. His lineup included Lindy Miller, who had failed to break par in only one tournament all spring; Tom Jones, an All-America as a freshman; Jaime Gonzales, "a Brazilian with a 26-inch waist and a heavyweight's golf game"; David Edwards; and freshman Britt Harrison, whom Holder called the best high school player in the country the year before. The Pokes had an additional edge: They were somewhat acclimated to the fierce New Mexico wind, "the kind that sends iron shots into the weeds and turns the greens into linoleum."

The Cowboys led by nine strokes heading into the final round. When the four top players turned the front nine a combined one over par, the outcome was settled. State won by seven strokes.

Maybe your experience with a juggernaut involved a game against a team full of major college prospects, a league tennis match against a former college player, or your presentation for the project you knew didn't stand a chance. Whatever it was, you've been slam-dunked before.

Being part of a juggernaut is certainly more fun than being in the way of one. Just ask OSU's opponents in that 1976 championship. Or consider the forces of evil aligned against God. At least the teams that took the field against the Pokes in Albuquerque had some hopes that they might win. No such hope exists for those who oppose God.

That's because their fate is already spelled out in detail. It's in the book; we all know how the story ends. God's enemies may talk big and bluster now, but they will be soundly trounced and routed in the most decisive defeat of all time.

You sure want to be on the winning side in that one.

*All this talk just puts more pressure on Wake Forest.*
*-- OSU's David Edwards on beating the juggernaut*

**The most lopsided victory in all of history**
**will be God's ultimate triumph over evil.**

# PRESSURE POINT

**Read 1 Kings 18:16-40.**

*"Answer me, O Lord, answer me, so these people will know that you, O Lord, are God" (v. 37).*

**N**o pressure," head coach Mike Gundy said. He was joking and he knew it.

The game of Sept. 5, 2009, was called "the most anticipated season opener in school history." Newly renovated Boone Pickens Stadium would be opened with due pomp and circumstance. The Cowboys would enter the game ranked No. 9 in the country, the program's highest preseason spot ever. And the opponent would be one of the linchpins of that conference to the south and the east: the 13th-ranked Georgia Bulldogs.

Buildup for the game began as soon as the 2008 season ended in the Holiday Bowl. In the spring, the Georgia fight song blared constantly in the Pokes' weight room. "I couldn't get it out of my head," said cornerback Perrish Cox.

Four hours before the game, a prominent OSU booster proclaimed this day to be the "biggest in the history of the university." That led to Gundy's quip, an admission of the immense pressure that burdened his shoulders and those of his players.

Georgia promptly took the opening kickoff and drove 80 yards for a touchdown. But the Cowboys took the suddenly ratcheted pressure in stride. "In years past we would have gone in the tank," Gundy admitted. This time was different, however. "After they scored, no one flinched," said the head Poke.

Instead, State dominated the Bulldogs defensively after that opening drive. Georgia would cross midfield only once the rest of the game. Late in the second quarter, free safety Lucien Antoine forced a fumble that cornerback Terrance Anderson fell on. That set up a field goal that gave OSU the lead for good at 10-7.

When Cox returned the second-half kickoff 73 yards, the subsequent TD made it 17-7. Georgia was done, having succumbed to the pressure of the Cowboy defense. State won 24-10.

Like the OSU athletic teams, you live every day with pressure. As Elijah did so long ago, you lay it on the line with everybody watching. Your family, coworkers, or employees – they depend on you. You know the pressure of a deadline, of a job evaluation, of taking the risk of asking someone to go out with you.

Help in dealing with daily pressure is readily available, and the only price you pay for it is your willingness to believe. God will give you the grace to persevere if you ask prayerfully.

And while you may need some convincing, the pressures of daily living are really small potatoes since they all will pass. The real pressure comes when you stare into the face of eternity because what you do with it is irrevocable and forever. You can handle that pressure easily enough by deciding for Jesus. Eternity is then taken care of; the pressure's off – forever.

*Pressure is for tires.*

-- *Charles Barkley*

**The greatest pressure you face in life
concerns where you will spend eternity,
which can be dealt with by deciding for Jesus.**

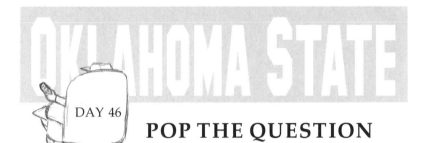

# POP THE QUESTION

**Read Matthew 16:13-17.**

*"'But what about you?' he asked. 'Who do you say I am?'" (v. 15)*

**O**SU head football coach Pat Jones was once asked a question so strikingly stupid that it was obvious to everyone in the room that the reporter was clueless.

In 1984, his first year at the helm in Stillwater, Jones coached the Cowboys to the first ten-win season in school history (including a win over South Carolina in the Gator Bowl) and finished in the top 10. "We knew we were going to be good," Jones said. "How good, we didn't know."

Jimmy Johnson, who took over the Miami Hurricane program, had not left the cupboard bare. The '83 team had gone 8-4, the four losses by a total of twelve points. Rusty Hilger, who went on to an eight-year career in the pros, was the quarterback. Leslie O'Neal and defensive back Rod Brown would earn All-America honors. Safety Mark Moore was a year away from the first of two All-American seasons. Thurman Thomas was a freshman.

Jones would find out just how good his team was right away. In his first-ever game as a college head coach, his Cowboys met Arizona State, which one publication had ranked No. 1 in its pre-season picks. State killed the Sun Devils 45-3, scoring the game's first 23 points. Jones said, "They couldn't move the ball on us and they couldn't tackle [Charles] Crawford," who had 137 yards rushing. "He literally ran wild on them," Jones gushed.

In the press conference after the game, one reporter from the West Coast unwittingly revealed that he had done no homework in preparation for the game. He asked Jones if this would rank as the biggest game of his career. The head coach politely pointed out that this was the first game of his career.

Life is an ongoing search for answers, and thus whether our life is lived richly or is wasted is largely determined by both the quality and the quantity of the answers we find. Life is indeed one question after another. What's for dinner? Can we afford a new car? What kind of team will OSU have this season?

But we also continuously seek answers to questions at another, more crucial level. What will I do with my life? Why am I here? Why does God allow suffering and tragedy?

An aspect of wisdom is reconciling ourselves to and being comfortable with the fact that we will never know all of the answers. Equally wise is the realization that the answers to life's more momentous questions lie within us, not beyond us.

One question overrides all others, the one Jesus asked Peter: "Who do you say I am?" Peter gave the one and only correct answer: "You are the Son of the Living God." How you answer that question is really the only one that matters, since it decides not just how you spend your life but how you spend eternity.

*[The reporter] acted like he knew that [it was my first game] and wrote it down, but he didn't know it.*
  *-- Pat Jones on the dumb question he was asked after the ASU game*

**Only one question in life determines
your eternal fate: Who do you say Jesus is?**

**DAY 47**

# BE PREPARED

**Read Matthew 10:5-23.**

*"I am sending you out like sheep among wolves. Therefore be as shrewd as snakes and as innocent as doves" (v. 16).*

The tailback didn't have his helmet. The quarterback was -- uh -- taking advantage of the facilities. The OSU first team just wasn't prepared to go back onto the field.

On Sept. 6, 2003, State coasted to a 48-24 win over Wyoming. With 6:36 left in the third quarter, the Cowboys led 41-7. At that point, head coach Les Miles decided to send his offensive starters to the sideline. "Time to rest. Let the kids play. Garbage time." So the first-teamers relaxed, their impressive work for the day over and done with. Or so they thought.

The second-team offense gained only two first downs on three possessions, all of which ended in punts. Meanwhile, Wyoming quickly scored ten points to make it a 41-17 game with 10:11 to play. Lots of time left and Miles envisioned only the worst-case scenario. "If the second team had made a mistake in our territory, it could have been a quick score, onsides kick and suddenly we're up seven and it's a heck of a ball game," said the boss Cowboy.

So he called for his starters to get back into the game, which turned out to be rather easier said than done. Starting tailback Tatum Bell had to hunt down his helmet. "I was over there chilling, just talking," Bell said. Somebody had to find quarterback Josh Fields, who was off making himself more comfortable. Almost no one was prepared to go into the game. Once all the scrambling was done, the first-team went out and did what Miles wanted: they scored again. Bell gained eight yards, Fields threw a 19-yard pass to wide receiver Gabe Lindsay, and Bell covered the last 34 yards with a pair of scampers. OSU led 48-17 with 8:21 to play. Game over. The starters now could honestly forget about being prepared.

You know the importance of preparation in your own life. You went to the bank for a car loan, facts and figures in hand. That presentation you made at work was seamless because you practiced. The kids' school play suffered no meltdowns because they rehearsed. Knowing what you need to do and doing what you must to succeed isn't luck; it's preparation.

Jesus understood this, and he prepared his followers by lecturing them and by sending them on field trips. Two thousand years later, the life of faith requires similar training and study. You prepare so you'll be ready when that unsaved neighbor standing beside you at your backyard grill asks about Jesus. You prepare so you will know how God wants you to live. You prepare so you are certain in what you believe when the secular, godless world challenges it.

And one day you'll see God face to face. You certainly want to be prepared for that.

*My mind was out of it until they told me to get back in.*
*-- Tatum Bell on preparing himself to go back into the Wyoming game*

**Living in faith requires constant study**
**and training, preparation for the day**
**when you meet God face to face.**

DAY 48

# DOWNRIGHT CRAZY

### Read Luke 13:31-35.

*"Some Pharisees came to Jesus and said to him, 'Leave this place and go somewhere else. Herod wants to kill you.' He replied, 'Go tell that fox . . . I must keep going today and tomorrow and the next day'" (vv. 31-33).*

In 1943, when Henry Iba took his team to New York City for a tour of the East, other coaches told him that he was crazy. Why? Because he put a player who was seven feet tall on the floor.

The prevailing philosophy among coaches in the 1940s was that basketball could not be played by men as big as Robert Kurland, who was almost 7'0". Even Iba had his reservations, but he liked the gangling player's attitude, and he took a chance.

The press, opposing players and coaches, and the fans heaped unprecedented abuse upon Kurland. One coach called him "a physical freak who was liable to ruin the game of basketball if he did not make a mockery of it first." That coach called Kurland a "glandular goon."

Because the military didn't have a uniform big enough to fit him, Kurland was never called into service during World War II. He was the only player from the '43 squad to return to Stillwater in 1944. Iba changed his whole defensive philosophy to take advantage of Kurland's height. He used a 1-1-3 zone with Kurland stationed under the goal. His job was simple: to be a goaltender, swatting away shot after shot. Iba also built his offense around his big man.

When Iba headed East in 1944, those same coaches who had questioned the head coach's sanity the year before realized that Kurland's emergence as a player had "initiated a revolution in the game of basketball."

Kurland led Oklahoma A&M to a pair of national championships in 1945 and '46. As a senior in 1946, he led the nation in scoring, setting a school record with 58 points against St. Louis. He was a three-time All-America and won the Helms Foundation Award in 1946 as the country's best college player.

What some see as crazy -- like playing Bob Kurland -- often is shrewd instead. Like the time you went into business for yourself or when you headed back to school. Maybe it was when you fixed up that old house. Or when you bought that new company's stock.

You know a good thing when you see it but are also shrewd enough to spot something that's downright crazy. Jesus was that way too. He knew that his entering Jerusalem was in complete defiance of all apparent reason and logic since a whole bunch of folks who wanted to kill him were waiting for him there.

Nevertheless, he went because he also knew that when the great drama had played out he would defeat not only his personal enemies but the most fearsome enemy of all: death itself.

It was, after all, a shrewd move that provided the way to your salvation.

*The sport was about to be surrendered to giants.*
*-- The effect Henry Iba's "crazy" decision had on basketball*

**It's so good it sounds crazy -- but it's not: through faith in Jesus, you can have eternal life with God.**

DAY 49

# GIFT-WRAPPED

**Read James 1:13-18.**

*"Every good and perfect gift is from above, coming down from the Father of the heavenly lights" (v. 17).*

Linda Simmons gave her husband a most precious gift: life.

Bob Simmons was Oklahoma State's head football coach from 1995-2000. In 1997, he was named the Big 12 Coach of the Year after leading the Cowboys to an 8-4 record.

During the season, though, problems with Simmons' kidneys worsened. Doctors speculated that years of stress has brought on their decline. A specialist told Simmons he should be on dialysis. Another bluntly told him that inside, he was a train wreck.

With a two-year wait in Oklahoma for a cadaver kidney, Simmons faced exhausting and time-consuming dialysis. A transplant from a living donor was his only hope for a normal life.

Simmons' wife, Linda, a universal donor and thus a perfect match, offered a kidney, but he resisted. He knew how dangerous the operation was and that it generally was worse on the donor. He also refused to consider other family members.

Finally, one November day, Linda lay flat on the floor in her empty bedroom and prayed for guidance. Was giving up a kidney what God wanted her to do? God answered with a "yes," and led her to Isaiah 41:10, a promise to uphold her.

Her husband could reject her offer, but he couldn't argue with God. In March 1998, the couple went under the knife. Before the procedure, Linda wanted to shout she was so joyful. "Because I knew, the miracle was at hand," she said.

It was. The surgeries went off without any problems. Bob was back at practice in eleven days, though Linda needed months for her life to return to normal. When the head coach rejoined his team, he couldn't describe his wife's sacrificial gift without breaking into tears.

Few of us will ever receive a gift that requires a sacrifice to equal that which Linda Simmons made. Still, while receiving a gift is always nice, giving has its pleasures too, doesn't it? The children's excitement on Christmas morning. That smile of pure delight on your spouse's face when you came up with a really cool anniversary present. Your dad's surprise that time you didn't give him a tie or socks. There really does seem to be something to this being more blessed to give than to receive.

No matter how generous we may be, though, we are grumbling misers compared to God, the greatest gift-giver of all. All the good things in our lives – every one of them – come from God. Friends, love, health, family, the air we breathe, the sun that warms us, even our very lives are all gifts from a profligate God. And here's the kicker: He even gives us eternal life with him through the gift of his son.

What in the world can we possibly give God in return? Our love and our life.

*I was trying to get him to understand this was a gift.*
*– Linda Simmons on giving a kidney to her husband*

**Nobody can match God for giving, but you can give him the gift of your love in appreciation.**

DAY 50

# LEVEL PLAYING FIELD

**Read Romans 3:21-26.**

*"There is no distinction, since all have sinned and fall short of the glory of God" (vv. 22b-23 NRSV).*

**M**en against boys. That's the way it was in the 1946 Sugar Bowl when the playing field clearly wasn't level.

All-American Bob Fenimore (See Devotions No. 25 and 91.) led Oklahoma A&M to an undefeated season in 1945, which earned the Aggies a berth in the Sugar Bowl. The opponent was the Gaels of St. Mary's. There was such a disparity in the two teams that when the California boys took the field for warmups, the crowd laughed because they were so small. Man-for-man, the Cowboys were 15 pounds heavier than the Gaels.

The disparity was more pronounced than mere size, however. With many of its players having not yet returned from active duty during World War II, the Gaels were the youngest team ever to play in the Sugar Bowl. Seven starters on the team were only 17.

On the other hand, Oklahoma State started seven war veterans. Fullback Jim Reynolds had flown fifty-two missions over Germany. Tackle Bert Cole had been shot down over Yugoslavia and spent seven months making his way back to Allied lines. This game was truly an instance of men against boys.

But the boys were pretty good. They hung tough, trailing only 14-13 at halftime. After that, though, A&M's size and strength took over the game. Fenimore returned a punt 43 yards to the St.

# COWBOYS

Mary's 7 and then scored on fourth down. The PAT was blocked. St. Mary's wasn't a real threat to score, but the score stayed 20-13 until the closing minutes. A fumble at the St. Mary's 35 set up a 1-yard Reynolds touchdown run. Then on A&M's next possession, a Reynolds pass was batted into the air by a defender, but reserve back Joe Thomas grabbed the deflection and scored.

On something less than a level playing field, the powerful and experienced Cowboys prevailed 33-13.

We should face up to one of life's basic facts: Its playing field isn't level. Others, it seems, get all the breaks. They get the cushy job; they win the lottery; their father owns the business. Some people – perhaps undeservedly -- just have it made.

That said, we just have to accept that the playing field isn't level and get over it. Dwelling on life's inequities can create only bitterness and cynicism, leading us to grumble about what we don't have while ignoring the blessings God continuously showers upon us. A moment's pause and reflection is all it takes for us to call to mind any number of friends, acquaintances, and strangers with whom we would not exchange situations.

The only place in life where we really stand on a level playing field is before God. There, all people are equal because we all need the lifeline God offers through Jesus — and we all have access to it.

*We looked like midgets on the field.*
*-- St. Mary's player Herman Wedemeyer on the '46 Sugar Bowl*

**Unlike life's playing field, God's playing field is level because everyone has equal access to what God has done through Jesus Christ.**

DAY 51

# REST EASY

**Read Hebrews 4:1-11.**

*"There remains, then, a Sabbath rest for the people of God; for anyone who enters God's rest also rests from his own work, just as God did from his. Let us, therefore, make every effort to enter that rest" (vv. 9-11).*

Vernand Morency was well known nationally as one of college football's premier running backs. Around the OSU campus and among his teammates, however, he was just as well known for sleeping in his cleats one night before a game.

After earning high-school All-American honors in both football and baseball, Morency signed with the Colorado Rockies and spent three years in the minors. He always insisted baseball was his best sport, "but every year schools were calling me to see if I was interested in coming back to football."

Morency became more interested in football as his baseball career topped out in Class A ball. One of his minor league teammates was former OSU star Matt Holliday, son of Cowboys baseball coach Tom Holliday. Matt hooked Morency up with State head football coach Les Miles, and in 2002, Morency became a 22-year-old freshman running back at Oklahoma State.

He played in six games in '02 before an ankle sprain sidelined him. In 2003, he was second on the team with 918 yards. His junior year was a breakout season; he led the Cowboys with 1,474 yards rushing. "We rolled the dice and basically designed our offense around him," said offensive coordinator Mike Gundy.

As Morency's fame spread so did the story of his bizarre sleepwear the eve of a game. The school newspaper reported that the night before the season-opening game against UCLA in 2004, Morency slept in his football shoes, cleats and all. He insisted he wasn't being superstitious. "I just wanted to try them on and break them in," he said.

He certainly was rested and ready for the game. He rushed for 261 yards and two touchdowns in the 31-20 win.

As part of the natural rhythm of life, rest -- with or without shoes -- is important to maintain physical health. Rest has different images, though: a good eight hours in the sack; a leisurely Saturday morning that begins in the backyard with the paper and a pot of coffee; a vacation in the mountains, where the most strenuous thing you do is change position in the hot tub.

Rest is also part of the rhythm and the health of our spiritual lives. Often we envision the faithful person as always busy, always doing something for God whether it's teaching Sunday school or showing up at church every time the doors open.

But God himself rested from work, and in blessing us with the Sabbath, he calls us into a time of rest. To rest by simply spending time in the presence of God is to receive spiritual revitalization and rejuvenation. Sleep refreshes your body and your mind; God's rest refreshes your soul.

*I don't understand, but I'm all for it if it works.*
*-- OSU coach Larry Porter on Vernand Morency's cleaty sleepwear*

**God promises you a spiritual rest
that renews and refreshes your soul.**

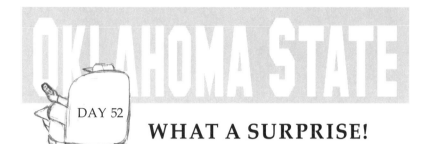

# WHAT A SURPRISE!

### Read 1 Thessalonians 5:1-11.

*"But you, brothers, are not in darkness so that this day should surprise you like a thief" (v. 4).*

Eddie Sutton's basketball team of 2003-04 was a big surprise. Described somewhat poetically as "a ragtag roster of transfers, junior college wanderers and injury-stricken sob stories," the Cowboys put together the greatest season OSU men's basketball had seen since Hank Iba's national champions in 1945 and 1946. They went 31-4, tying the school record for wins in a season set originally by those '46 champions. They advanced to the semifinals in the NCAA Tournament before suffering a heartbreaking two-point loss on a basket with 1.5 seconds left.

Nobody really expected it. The squad was the consensus pick to finish fifth in the league behind Texas, Kansas, Oklahoma, and Missouri. Instead, they went 5-1 against that group.

The highlight of the season came on March 2 with a showdown between the 8th-ranked Cowboys and the 10th-ranked Longhorns of Texas for the Big 12 Conference title. In a nationally televised game, OSU shot 64 percent the last half and won 76-67.

That win set the stage for what was an anti-climactic but still an exciting night against Texas A&M on March 6. The Aggies were 0-15 in the league and had won only seven games all season, so a Cowboy win was a foregone conclusion. The suspense lasted only a few minutes, and OSU coasted to a 70-41 victory.

The crowd lingered after the game to cheer on the players and the coaches as they cut down the nets and received the Big 12 trophy. This most pleasant surprise of a team had won OSU's first outright conference title in 39 years. Even some of the players were surprised. "I'm kind of speechless right now," said senior forward Ivan McFarlin. "I never thought this would happen."

Surprise birthday parties are a delight. And what's the fun of opening Christmas presents when we already know what's in them? Some surprises in life provide us with experiences that are both joyful and delightful.

Generally, though, we expend energy and resources to avoid most surprises and the impact they may have upon our lives. We may be surprised by the exact timing of a baby's arrival, but we nevertheless have the bags packed beforehand and the nursery all set for its occupant. Paul used this very image (v. 3) to describe the Day of the Lord, when Jesus will return to claim his own and establish his kingdom. We may be caught by surprise, but we must still be ready.

The consequences of being caught unprepared by a baby's insistence on being born are serious indeed. They pale, however, beside the eternal effects of not being ready when Jesus returns. We prepare ourselves just as Paul told us to (v. 8): We live in faith, hope, and love, ever on the alert for that great, promised day.

*These guys have certainly surprised me the way they continue to grow as a team.*
*-- Head coach Eddie Sutton on his 2003-04 Big 12 champions*

**The timing of Jesus' return will be a surprise;
the consequences should not be.**

# JUST PERFECT

**Read Matthew 5:43-48.**

*"Be perfect, therefore, as your heavenly Father is perfect"*
*(v. 48).*

One writer called it "a perfect start for the Cowboys." It was truly an apt beginning as for one incredible half, State fans watched OSU play about as perfectly as any football team ever could.

As of Oct. 13, 2007, State had lost to Nebraska twenty straight times in Lincoln. True, the Huskers were struggling at 4-2, but the Cowboys weren't any better at 3-3. Nobody saw what was coming because nobody saw perfection.

That perfect start? The Cowboy defense forced the Cornhuskers into three-and-out on their opening possession. Then the offense took the ball 50 yards in eight plays with senior Julius Crosslin scoring from the 1 after a 21-yard catch by Adarius Bowman. 7-0.

But then to everyone's amazement -- particularly the Nebraska fans -- the perfection continued on through the first 30 minutes of the game. At halftime, "the stat sheet was replete with remarkable numbers." For instance, the Cowboys had 357 yards to Nebraska's 101. State ran 42 plays, 29 them of them in Husker territory. Tailback Dantrell Savage rushed for 148 yards, which qualified as his career best. He would finish with 212 yards.

The most perfect part of that first half? The score. State led 38-0. Never in its long and storied history had Nebraska allowed 38 points in the first half to anyone at home.

Any thoughts the Huskers had of a comeback were dispelled by one sequence in that perfect half. NU drove to the State 10, but on fourth down safety Andre Sexton and linebacker Jeremy Nethon dropped the Husker runner for no gain. OSU then drove 90 yards in six plays, freshman tailback Kendall Hunter scoring on a 33-yard romp. That made it 24-0 instead of 17-7.

And the final score? A close-to-perfect 45-14.

Nobody's perfect; we all make mistakes every day. We botch our personal relationships; at work we seek competence, not perfection. To insist upon personal or professional perfection in our lives is to establish an impossibly high standard that will eventually destroy us physically, emotionally, and mentally.

Yet that is exactly the standard God sets for us. Our love is to be perfect, never ceasing, never failing, never qualified – just the way God loves us. And Jesus didn't limit his command to only preachers and goody-two-shoes types. All of his disciples are to be perfect as they navigate their way through the world's ambiguous definition and understanding of love.

But that's impossible! Well, not necessarily, if to love perfectly is to serve God wholeheartedly and to follow Jesus with single-minded devotion. Anyhow, in his perfect love for us, God makes allowance for our imperfect love and the consequences of it in the perfection of Jesus.

*If we chase perfection, we can catch excellence.*

*-- Vince Lombardi*

**In his perfect love for us, God provides a way
for us to escape the consequences
of our imperfect love for him: Jesus.**

# BAD IDEA

**Read Mark 14:43-50.**

*"The betrayer had arranged a signal with them: 'The one I kiss is the man; arrest him and lead him away under guard'" (v. 44).*

**A**fter Jimmy Johnson and Pat Jones were hired at Oklahoma State, they decided to stay on at Pitt to coach in the bowl game. Bad idea.

Johnson was the last candidate brought in for an interview in the search to succeed Jim Stanley in 1978. The assistant head coach and the defensive coordinator for Jackie Sherrill, Johnson made such an impression on the interview committee that they told him to stick around another day. He called his buddy Jones back in Pittsburgh and told him he was going to have to buy some more clothes because he hadn't packed enough for another day.

Johnson and Jones had known each other since college days and had coached together at Arkansas. When Johnson landed the interview in Stillwater, he asked Jones if he wanted to go with him if he got the job and coach his defense. On the spot, Jones said yes.

When the announcement came that the two were headed to Oklahoma State, they told Sherrill they would stay on to coach through the Tangerine Bowl. It was not a good idea.

During the week before the bowl game, Johnson tried to convince two other Pitt assistants to join him at State. At the same time, Sherrill was trying to talk them into staying. As Jones put it, the situation "got a bit sticky." It got so sticky that the coaches wound up having two separate staff meetings, one with the guys who were leaving and one with the guys who were staying. "It was really a little bit tense," Jones said.

The situation deteriorated so badly that when Johnson and Jones changed clothes in the dressing room after the bowl game (a loss), one of the Pitt equipment managers stood by and watched to make sure they didn't swipe any gear.

That sure-fire investment you made from a pal's hot stock tip. The expensive exercise machine that now traps dust bunnies under your bed. Blond hair. Telling your wife you wanted to eat at the restaurant with the waitresses in the skimpy shorts. They seemed like pretty good ideas at the time; they weren't.

We all have bad ideas in our lifetime. They provide us with some of our most painful experiences. If we learn from them, though, they can also be among our most valuable experiences.

Some ideas, however, are so irreparably and inherently bad that we cannot help but wonder why they were even conceived in the first place. Almost two thousand years ago a man had just such an idea. Judas' betrayal of Jesus remains to this day one of the most heinous acts of treachery in history.

Turning his back on Jesus was a bad idea for Judas then; it's a bad idea for us now.

*That taught us that, if you can, you need to get on down the road.*
*— Pat Jones on the bad idea of staying on at Pitt to coach the bowl game*

**We all have some bad ideas in our lives; nothing equals the folly of turning away from Jesus.**

# HAVE A GOOD DAY

**Read Psalm 34.**

*"Whoever of you loves life and desires to see many good days, keep your tongue from evil and your lips from speaking lies" (vv. 12-13).*

A linebacker had to pray for breath he was celebrating so hard; the quarterback was feeling weird and then set a school record. Man, it was a blessed day to be a Cowboy.

The 4-5 Cowboys of 2002 traveled to Lawrence to take on Kansas on Nov. 16 with bowl hopes still alive. Before the game started, sophomore quarterback Josh Fields wasn't sure it was going to be such a good day. He was feeling "weird," as he put it. He just wasn't himself, feeling "loose," "really relaxed," and "just kind of goofy."

He should have felt that way more often. Fields went out and set a school record by throwing six touchdown passes for 354 yards, the third best day in OSU history. He was sacked only once and didn't throw an interception, completing 17 of 27 passes. The Cowboys shot down the Jayhawks 55-20.

Perhaps the most exciting play of this good day for the Cowboys came from senior linebacker Terrence Robinson. Early in the fourth quarter, he picked up a fumble recovery and went 93 yards for a touchdown that made it a 55-17 game. That was a very long way for the 240-pounder to run.

"I thought it was going to take me an hour-and-a-half," he said.

# COWBOYS

After the first 20 yards, "My legs started feeling tired, my body was feeling weird -- I started feeling like I was an 80-year-old man." It got worse after he finally lumbered into the end zone and his teammates jumped on him in celebration. "It was one of those moments where, 'Oh, please, if I could just take another breath, thank you, Lord,'" Robinson said.

He got his breath, Fields got his record, the Cowboys got their win and later their bowl game. It was a blessed day all around.

It's commonplace today. Someone performs a service for you – a counter clerk, a waiter, a porter – and their parting shot is a cheerful, "Have a good day!" It's the world's wish for us as if it is the culmination of everything the world has to offer.

For those who put their faith and their trust in the world, it is. They can't hope for anything better because they turn to an inadequate source.

There is something much better, however, than a mere "good" day. It's a "blessed" day. It's a day that, as the psalmist envisions it, is much more than simply managing to make it through twenty-four hours without a catastrophe or heartbreak. It's a day in which God manifests his goodness by pouring out blessings upon us.

How do we transform a routine "good" day into an awesome "blessed" day? We trust and obey almighty God rather than the machinations and the people of this world. For God, having a good day simply isn't good enough. For us, it shouldn't be either.

*It's a great day for [Josh] Fields.*
*-- Head coach Les Miles on what was a blessed day for OSU*

**The world offers a good day;**
**God offers a blessed day.**

# ROCK SOLID

**Read Luke 6:46-49.**

*"I will show you what he is like who comes to me and hears my words and puts them into practice. He is like a man building a house, who dug down deep and laid the foundation on rock" (vv. 47-48).*

The foundation for the sports dynasty that is the Oklahoma State wrestling program was laid by a man who never wrestled competitively.

Ed Gallagher was among the best of the early athletes at Oklahoma A&M. He set school records in the 100-yard dash and the hurdles. In 1908, he set a record that still stands, breaking a 99-yard touchdown run from scrimmage against Kansas.

After graduating and spending two years away from A&M, Gallagher returned as athletic director. During his absence, A.M. Colville had started the wrestling program. In 1915, Gallagher took it over despite never having wrestled in an organized program in high school or college.

As an engineer, Gallagher applied a systematic approach to the sport. He even selected a particular type of young man, sons of "upstanding" parents and "boys who cannot go out in society." That is, he looked for boys with character and not much money who could use wrestling as a springboard to success.

Gallagher expected his wrestlers "to live clean -- no smoking, no drinking, and, perhaps most startling nowadays, no dating."

As the coach put it, "The best woman in the world can do you no good." And, no, he wasn't a bachelor; he married right out of college and had six children.

Gallagher's record was astounding. He coached until he collapsed and died while on vacation; he was 53. His Cowboys were 136-5-4, an overall winning percentage of .952. Of his 24 seasons, 19 were undefeated and eleven of them were national champions.

Like the Oklahoma State wrestling program, your life is an ongoing project, a work in progress. As with any complex construction job, if your life is to be stable, it must have a solid foundation, which holds everything up and keeps everything together.

R. Alan Culpepper said in *The New Interpreter's Bible*, "We do not choose whether we will face severe storms in life; we only get to choose the foundation on which we will stand." In other words, tough times are inevitable. If your foundation isn't rock-solid, you will have nothing on which to stand as those storms buffet you, nothing to keep your life from flying apart into a cycle of disappointment and destruction.

But when the foundation is solid and sure, you can take the blows, stand strong, recover, and live with joy and hope. Only one foundation is sure and foolproof: Jesus Christ. Everything else you build upon will fail you.

*[OSU] has built a wrestling legacy unmatched by any other college wrestling program. The man who laid the foundation is Ed Gallagher.*
-- Mark Palmer, revwrestling.com

**In the building of your life, you must start with a foundation in Jesus Christ, or the first trouble that shows up will knock you down.**

# UNBELIEVABLE!

### Read Hebrews 3:7-19.

*"See to it, brothers, that none of you has a sinful, unbelieving heart that turns away from the living God" (v. 12).*

**S**ince OSU had never beaten a nationally ranked Nebraska team, it was quite believable that the Cornhuskers would lead 16-0. What was unbelievable is that the Cowboys would outscore the boys from Lincoln 41-7 after that.

The Huskers were ranked 20th when they rolled into Boone Pickens Stadium on Oct. 28, 2006. That apparently amounted to the kiss of death for the Cowboys, who indeed had never beaten a Nebraska team when it was sitting somewhere in the polls. The rather unfortunate streak was apparently about to be extended when Nebraska jumped out to a 16-0 lead in the second quarter.

This band of Cowboys was accustomed to being behind and pulling off big rallies, however. After all, they had squashed Kansas two weeks before after trailing 17-0. But this was Nebraska.

It didn't matter.

What the Cowboys did to the Cornhuskers was simply unbelievable. They went on a 41-7 run, allowing Nebraska a meaningless touchdown with only seven seconds left in the 41-29 win. By then, OSU fans and players had long since begun celebrating.

One writer called the comeback the "most important home triumph since the 2002 Bedlam win over Oklahoma." (See Devo-

**COWBOYS**

tion No. 20.) Head coach Mike Gundy was less hyperbolic. "It's a good day for Oklahoma State," he said.

Tailback Dantrell Savage ran for 117 yards and two TDs, and Bobby Reid passed for 229 yards and two scores, one each to freshman tailback Keith Toston and wide receiver Adarius Bowman. Nebraska held a shaky 23-20 lead at halftime, "but the Cowboy offense had found its rhythm. Nebraska was doomed."

So, unbelievably, was the streak.

Much of what taxes the limits of our belief system has little effect on our lives. Maybe we don't believe in UFOs, honest politicians, aluminum baseball bats, Sasquatch, or the viability of electric cars. A healthy dose of skepticism is a natural defense mechanism that helps protect us in a world that all too often has designs on taking advantage of us.

That's not the case, however, when Jesus and God are part of the mix. Quite unbelievably, we often hear people blithely assert they don't believe in God. Or brazenly declare they believe in God but don't believe Jesus was anything but a good man and a great teacher.

At this point, unbelief becomes dangerous because God doesn't fool around with scoffers. He locks them out of the Promised Land, which isn't a country in the Middle East but Heaven itself.

Given that scenario, it's downright unbelievable that anyone would not believe.

*We knew (the Cowboys) were a great second-half team.*
*-- Husker head coach Bill Callahan, believing OSU could come back*

**Perhaps nothing is as unbelievable as that some people insist on not believing in God or his son.**

# THE LAST WORD

**Read Luke 9:22-27.**

*"The Son of Man . . . must be killed and on the third day be raised to life. . . . [S]ome who are standing here will . . . see the kingdom of God" (vv. 22, 27).*

The Sooners did the talking early, but the Cowboys had the last word.

Bedlam 2011 offered the usual intensity with the additional factor of deciding the Big 12 championship. Sooner head coach Bob Stoops started the talk early in the week by declaring that his team should be the league's "one true champion" if it beat the Cowboys though that would create a three-way tie at the top.

The talking and strutting continued before the Dec. 3 game. When the Sooners gathered at the middle of the field after their warmups, some of them pointed and gestured toward the OSU fans. Minutes later, about a dozen Sooners ran down to the tunnel through which the OSU players would trot onto the field so they could confront them. The game officials and some of their coaches, including Stoops, chased them back to the bench area.

After that, though, all the talking belonged to the Cowboys as they dropped a monumental bomb on the heads of the hapless Sooners, routing them 44-10. Brandon Weeden hit Tracy Moore on a crossing pattern for a 53-yard play that set up a six-yard scoring run by Jeremy Smith. After a field goal, the Cowboys "put the Sooners out of their misery" in a span of roughly eight minutes. The game was essentially over by halftime with State leading 24-3. The showdown turned into a blowout in the third quarter when the Pokes tacked on 20 more points.

After the game, "the locker room was the happiest ever seen in Oklahoma State history." The jubilant winners held, hugged, and even kissed their championship trophy.

Some of the Sooners may have had something to say before the game, but the Cowboys ultimately had the last word, the only one that mattered: Big 12 Champions!

Why is it that we often come up with the last word – the perfect zinger -- only long after the incident that called for a smart and pithy rejoinder is over? "Man, I shoulda said that! That woulda fixed his wagon!" But it's too late.

Nobody in history, though, including us, could ever hope to match the man who had the greatest last word of them all: Jesus Christ. His enemies killed him and put him in a tomb, confident they were done with that nuisance for good. Instead, they were unwitting participants in God's great plan of redemption, unintentionally giving the last word to Jesus. He has it still.

Jesus didn't go to that cross so he could die; he went to that cross so all those who follow him might live. Because of Jesus' own death on the cross, the final word for us is not our own death. Rather it is life, through our salvation in Jesus Christ.

*All week I said [to his offensive line], 'We're going to win this game because of you guys.'*
*-- Brandon Weeden on the talking he did before Bedlam 2011*

**With Jesus, the last word is always life
and is never death.**

DAY 59

# THE FAME GAME

### Read 1 Kings 10:1-10, 18-29.

*"King Solomon was greater in riches and wisdom than all the other kings of the earth. The whole world sought audience with Solomon" (vv. 23-24).*

**S**hawn Mackey didn't achieve fame and fortune as an all-conference or All-American player. He did, however, make one of the more famous plays in Cowboy history.

The 1987 John Hancock Sun Bowl featured the 11th-ranked Cowboys and the Mountaineers from West Virginia. "One of the most entertaining games of the 1987-88 bowl season" was played on a cold and snowy Christmas Day. State fielded a team loaded with talent. Mike Gundy was the quarterback, wide receiver Hart Lee Dykes his prime target. Thurman Thomas and Barry Sanders were both on the field for the Pokes.

Thomas scored twice to stake State to a 14-7 first-quarter lead, but in the second period, the Mountaineers scored 17 unanswered points for a 24-14 halftime lead.

In the third quarter, after another Thomas touchdown and a WVa field goal, Gundy hit J.R. Dillard with a touchdown pass for a 28-27 State lead. The game's MVP, Thomas scored his fourth TD for a late 35-27 OSU lead, but the Mountaineers hurried downfield and scored with 1:13 to pull within two at 35-33. The try for the two-point conversion was a no-brainer.

A redshirt freshman, Mackey was on the defensive line. He

would start his next two seasons but would wreck a knee in the final game of his junior year. He decided not to play his senior season because, as he put it, his heart wasn't in it.

On the two-point try, Harris completed a pass to his tight end, but Mackey tackled him just shy of the goal line. His famous play preserved the 35-33 Sun-Bowl win for the Cowboys.

Have you ever wanted to be famous? Hanging out with other rich and famous people, having folks with microphones listen to what you say, throwing money around like toilet paper, meeting adoring and clamoring fans, signing autographs, and posing for the paparazzi before you climb into your imported sports car?

Many of us yearn to be famous, well-known in the places and by the people that we believe matter. That's all fame amounts to: strangers knowing your name and your face.

The truth is that you are already famous where it really does matter, which excludes TV's talking heads, screaming teenagers, rapt moviegoers, or D.C. power brokers. You are famous because Almighty God knows your name, your face, and everything else there is to know about you.

If a persistent photographer snapped you pondering this fame – the only kind that has eternal significance – would the picture show the world unbridled joy or the shell-shocked expression of a mug shot?

*That was my 15 seconds of fame.*
*— Shawn Mackey on his clutch tackle in the '87 Sun Bowl*

**You're already famous because God
knows your name and your face,
which may be either reassuring or terrifying.**

# GOOD SPORTS

**Read Titus 2:1-8.**

*"Show integrity, seriousness and soundness of speech that cannot be condemned, so that those who oppose you may be ashamed because they have nothing bad to say about us" (vv. 7b, 8).*

**H**enry Iba once engaged in an act of sportsmanship that may have cost his team a berth in the Final Four and thus a shot at the national title.

On a golf course in 1957, Iba, who doubled as State's athletic director, was invited to the upcoming Big Seven business meeting. The tacit understanding with the invitation was that Oklahoma State was to be admitted into the conference that would then become the Big Eight. At the meeting, representatives from the seven member schools voted unanimously to admit OSU into their exclusive club. They determined that the Pokes would begin league basketball play in 1959 and football competition in 1960.

Iba hoped that the Missouri Valley Conference, of which the school had been a member since 1925, would allow his basketball team to play a league schedule in 1957-58. At the time, invitation to the NCAA Tournament largely depended upon winning a conference championship. The league balked, though, and OSU thus played the season as an independent.

Led by 6'8" Arlen Clark, a natural forward forced to play center because no other starter exceeded six feet, the team lost five MVC games and wouldn't have won the conference. But they won 19 games, which teamed with wins over top-ranked Kansas and highly ranked Cincinnati to land the Cowboys in the tournament.

In the second round, Kansas State met Cincinnati, and the Wildcat coach asked Iba for advice on how to stop Oscar Robertson. Iba obliged. K State won and then beat OSU in the regional finals. Asked why he had helped K State when he would have been better off playing Cincinnati, Iba replied, "We are in the same conference with Kansas State now, and we must be friends."

One of life's paradoxes is that many who would never consider cheating on the tennis court or the racquetball court to gain an advantage think nothing of doing so in other areas of their life. The good sportsmanship they practice on the golf course or even on the Monopoly board doesn't carry over. They play with the truth, cut corners, abuse others verbally, run roughshod over the weak and the helpless, and generally cheat whenever they can to gain an advantage on the job or in their personal relationships.

But good sportsmanship is a way of living, not just of playing. Shouldn't you accept defeat without complaint (You don't have to like it.); win gracefully without gloating; treat your competition with fairness, courtesy, generosity, and respect? That's the way one team treats another in the name of sportsmanship. That's the way one person treats another in the name of Jesus.

*One person practicing sportsmanship is better than 100 teaching it.*
*-- Knute Rockne*

**Sportsmanship -- treating others with courtesy,**
**fairness, and respect -- is a way of living,**
**not just a way of playing.**

DAY 61

# GREAT EXPECTATIONS

**Read John 1:43-51.**

*"'Nazareth! Can anything good come from there?'*
*Nathanael asked" (v. 46).*

**D**an Bailey had virtually no expectations for himself when he arrived in Stillwater in 2007. He should have. He left as the top scorer in Cowboy football history.

Bailey showed up for his first practice as a nonscholarshipped walk-on kicker, and he wasn't really hoping for much. "I thought if I worked hard and stuck with it, I'd play two years, maybe," he said as his remarkable career at OSU wound down in 2010. "I didn't know if [I'd] be doing kickoffs or field goals or whatever." That "whatever" turned out to be the placekicking for four OSU seasons.

When Bailey drove his last kick through the uprights in the 2010 Alamo Bowl, a 36-10 win over Arizona, he had scored 370 points. He had converted 57 field goals and 199 PATs, missing only one. Those 370 points eclipsed Barry Sanders' 330 points as the most in school history.

Bailey won the Lou Groza Collegiate Place-Kicker Award as the best collegiate kicker in the country his senior season. The Associated Press named him Second-Team All-America.

One of the highlights of Bailey's unexpected career came on national television in 2010 when he kicked a 40-yard field goal on the final play to propel the Cowboys to a 38-35 win over Texas

A&M. "I just remember turning around and hugging my holder (Wes Harlan)," Bailey recalled. "Then getting tackled by everyone. It went through, and I just wanted to celebrate."

Head coach Mike Gundy was nonplussed about Bailey's game-winning kick, saying it simply met the expectations everyone had for him. "We expect him to make it, and he expects to make it," he said.

The blind date your friend promised would look like Brad Pitt or Jennifer Aniston but resembled a Munster or Cousin Itt. Your vacation that went downhill after the lost luggage. Often your expectations are raised only to be dashed. Sometimes it's best not to get your hopes up; then at least you have the possibility of being surprised as Dan Bailey was.

Worst of all, perhaps, is when you realize that you are the one not meeting others' expectations. The fact is, though, that you aren't here to live up to what others think of you. Jesus didn't; in part, that's why they killed him. But he did meet God's expectations for his life, which was all that really mattered.

Because God's kingdom is so great, God does have great expectations for any who would enter, and you should not take them lightly. What the world expects from you is of no importance; what God expects from you is paramount.

*To play four years and to have success as a team those four years, it's exceeded any expectations I had.*
*-- Dan Bailey*

**You have little, if anything, to gain from meeting the world's expectations of you; you have all of eternity to gain from meeting God's.**

# THE NIGHTMARE

**Read Mark 5:1-20.**

*"What do you want with me, Jesus, Son of the Most High God? Swear to God that you won't torture me!" (v. 7)*

Tulsa head coach Dave Rader had a recurring nightmare. It featured David Thompson running into daylight over and past his beleaguered defenders. It came true.

Rader was clearly apprehensive about OSU's senior tailback as the meeting with the Cowboys on Sept. 14, 1996, neared. The coach had long been aware of Thompson's talent. Five years before, he had "told anyone who would listen" that Thompson was the best high-school back in the state.

Now, he had a rather odd game tape to review for instruction as he prepared to stop Thompson. In the '96 season opener, OSU had eked out a 23-20 win over Division 1-AA Southwest Missouri State. Thompson had managed a grand total of 42 yards.

To replicate that feat, Rader let his safeties creep up to the line and dare the Cowboys to throw. OSU didn't take the hint. Instead, "the Cowboys were smartly stubborn and continued to pump the ball" to Thompson.

Rader's nightmare came true. Thompson ran around, over, and through the Hurricanes for 252 yards on 34 carries. He scored twice in the Cowboys' 30-9 win. At the time, that was the tenth-best rushing day in OSU history, the most yards since Gerald Hudson rolled up 246 yards against Missouri in 1990.

"How did they do that?" Rader asked in wonderment about Southwest Missouri's success against Thompson. He was left to admit, "Thompson had a great game" against his Hurricanes. The Tulsa head man wasn't the only coach the All-Big 12 back gave nightmares to. In his last game as a Cowboy, a 37-17 defeat of Baylor, Thompson rushed for 321 yards. He finished his career with 4,314 yards, the third-best total in OSU history, behind only Thurman Thomas and Terry Miller.

Falling. Drowning. Standing naked in a room crowded with fully dressed people. They're nightmares, dreams that jolt us from our sleep in anxiety or downright terror. The film industry has used our common nightmares to create horror movies that allow us to experience our fears vicariously. This includes the formulaic "evil vs. good" movies in which demons and the like render good virtually helpless in the face of their power and ruthlessness.

The spiritual truth, though, is that it is evil that has come face to face with its worst nightmare in Jesus. We seem to understand that our basic mission as Jesus' followers is to further his kingdom and change the world through emulating him in the way we live and love others. But do we appreciate that in truly living for Jesus, we are daily tormenting the very devil himself?

Satan and his lackeys quake helplessly in fear before the power of almighty God that is in us through Jesus.

*Dave Rader's worst nightmare was David Thompson running all over the Lewis Field turf.*
    *-- Sportswriter John Klein prior to the '96 OSU-Tulsa game*

**As the followers of Jesus Christ,
we are the stuff of Satan's nightmares.**

DAY 63

# TIME FOR A CHANGE

**Read Romans 6:1-14.**

*"Just as Christ was raised from the dead through the glory of the Father, we too may live a new life" (v. 4).*

When John Corker tells of how Jesus Christ can change lives, people listen because he knows firsthand of that power.

For Corker, the Heart of Dallas Bowl on Jan. 1, 2013, in which Oklahoma State blasted Purdue 58-14, was more than just a game. At OSU, Corker was an All-American linebacker and the Big Eight Defensive Player of the Year in 1978. He spent four seasons in the NFL and then played some arena ball and in the old USFL.

Not long after his football career was over, Corker had nothing except a cocaine habit that had taken all those thousand-dollar paychecks. He wound up homeless on the streets of Baltimore. "I was weighing about 180 pounds then, and my entire day was consisting of trying to come up with more money to smoke more coke," he said. He ate whatever he could find in dumpsters.

His brother took him to Texas, and he got a job driving a tractor-trailer. On a trip to Georgia with $100,000 worth of electronics, he stopped in Fort Worth to get high and couldn't remember where he parked. He searched desperately, but he never found the semi.

With no money and no job, he wandered into a Salvation Army shelter planning to stay one night. He stayed eight months as he experienced the awesome power Jesus Christ has to change lives.

Seven drug-free years later, on the morning of the bowl game, he told his story at a drug-rehabilitation facility and then hurried to Cotton Bowl Stadium to watch the Cowboys, the guest of the father of OSU starting center Evan Epstein. The game was special because Corker saw his former team play, but it was much more personal than that for him. Proceeds from the game go toward providing permanent residences for the homeless in Dallas.

The game, thus, was living proof of the message that Corker delivers based on his own life and faith: "There is hope."

Anyone who asserts no change is needed in his or her life just isn't paying attention. Every life has doubt, worry, fear, failure, frustration, unfulfilled dreams, and unsuccessful relationships in some combination. The memory and consequences of our past often haunt and trouble us.

Simply recognizing the need for change in our lives, though, doesn't mean the changes that will bring about hope, joy, peace, and fulfillment will occur. We need some power greater than ourselves or we wouldn't be where we are.

So where can we turn to? Where lies the hope for a changed life? It lies in an encounter with the Lord of all Hope: Jesus Christ. For a life turned over to Jesus, change is inevitable. With Jesus in charge, the old self with its painful and destructive ways of thinking, feeling, loving, and living is transformed.

A changed life is always only a talk with Jesus away.

*The Lord has made me a torchbearer. It can be done. You can get your life back. You can become productive in society again.*
*-- John Corker*

**In Jesus lie the hope and the power
that change lives.**

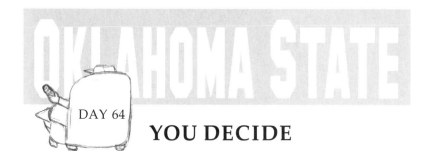

# YOU DECIDE

**Read John 6:60-69.**

*"The words I have spoken to you are spirit and they are life. Yet there are some of you who do not believe" (vv. 63b-64a).*

For three minutes, Cowgirl players, coaches, and fans waited on a decision from the referees while they studied video replays. When the decision came, it was a big one for OSU.

On March 23, the 26-7 OSU women's basketball team and the FSU Seminoles met in the second round of the 2008 NCAA Tournament. They played one of the most exciting games OSU fans had ever seen.

The contest was close all the way through. The Cowgirls never led by more than five points, the Seminoles never by more than four. The score was tied seventeen times; they swapped the lead twenty times. OSU senior guard Danielle Green bailed the Cowgirls out by converting a layup with 13.8 seconds left for a tie at 65. When FSU missed a desperate shot, it was on to overtime.

The Cowgirls took a five-point lead late in the extra period, but FSU rallied to tie it at 72 with 17.7 seconds left. To no one's surprise, OSU put the ball in the hands of sophomore Andrea Riley, the All-Big 12 point guard who as a senior would win the Nancy Lieberman Award as the best point guard in the country.

Riley dribbled the time away and then moved up and in for a shot. Just as the clock hit 0:00, she was fouled. But did the contact occur before or after time ran out? That was the decision the refs had to make as they hovered over the video replay. Time dragged on with the Cowgirls hoping for a chance to win it, the Seminoles hoping for another overtime. Finally, the officials decided; the foul had indeed occurred with 0.7 seconds on the clock.

Riley missed the first charity shot before she hit the second for the 73-72 OSU win. With a big boost from the refs' decision, the Cowgirls were on their way to the Sweet 16.

The decisions you have made along the way have shaped your life at every pivotal moment. Some decisions you made suddenly and carelessly; some you made carefully and deliberately; some were forced upon you. You may have discovered that some of those spur-of-the-moment decisions have turned out better than your carefully considered ones.

Of all your life's decisions, however, none is more important than one you cannot ignore: What have you done with Jesus? Even in his time, people chose to follow Jesus or to reject him, and nothing has changed; the decision must still be made and nobody can make it for you. Ignoring Jesus won't work either; that is, in fact, a decision, and neither he nor the consequences of your decision will go away.

Carefully considered or spontaneous, suddenly or gradually – how you arrive at a decision for Jesus doesn't matter; all that matters is that you get there.

*The officials are the authority on the court.*
*-- FSU head coach Sue Semrau on the decision to put 0.7 on the clock*

**A decision for Jesus may be spontaneous or considered; what counts is that you make it.**

# PROVE IT!

### Read Matthew 3.

*"But John tried to deter him, saying, 'I need to be baptized by you, and do you come to me?'" (v. 14)*

Tarrell Knauls believed he was good enough to play big-time football, but he had to prove it. He found an unusual way to do that: He dunked a basketball.

Knauls was not highly recruited, so he figured he'd play some college football at a smaller school, missing out on the big-time game. Then one day, OSU head coach Bob Simmons showed up -- at a basketball practice.

The head Cowpoke wasn't there by accident. Knauls' name had come up the summer before when assistant coach Mike Gundy watched him in a camp. Gundy told Simmons that Knauls was an athlete worth keeping an eye on. Simmons reviewed some film and agreed. "This guy could be a pretty good football player if he would invest some time in it," he said.

While Simmons was in town to watch R.W. McQuarters, who would be one of the most versatile players in OSU history, he decided to take a look at Knauls. The head Cowboy believed that watching a football player on the basketball court was a good way to evaluate his athletic skills, so he stopped by basketball practice.

Figuring he had to prove himself, Knauls decided to show off. "You know how that is when you see a coach up there and stuff, so I kind of did a little razzle-dazzle on a dunk," he said.

Simmons was duly impressed. "I just saw him go up, up and up and I just said, 'hmmmm,'" the coach said. The slam proved Knauls' athletic ability enough to land him a scholarship.

Knauls indeed was good enough. He was a three-year letterman and a two-year starter at linebacker for the Cowboys. As a senior in 1999, the AP named him All-Big 12.

Like Tarrell Knauls, you, too, have to prove yourself over and over again in your life. To your teachers, to that guy you'd like to date, to your parents, to your bosses, to the loan officer. It's always the same question: "Am I good enough?" Practically everything we do in life is aimed at proving that we are.

And yet, when it comes down to the most crucial situation in our lives, the answer is always a decisive and resounding "No!" Are we good enough to measure up to God? To deserve our salvation? John the Baptist knew he wasn't, and he was not only Jesus' relative but God's hand-chosen prophet. If he wasn't good enough, what chance do we have?

The notion that only "good" people can be church members is a perversion of Jesus' entire ministry. Nobody is good enough – without Jesus. Everybody is good enough – with Jesus. That's not because of anything we have done for God, but because of what he has done for us. We have nothing to prove to God.

*I knew that my heart was big enough and if I could get out there, I could tangle with the best of them.*
*-- Tarrell Knauls on proving himself.*

**The bad news is we can't prove to God's satisfaction how good we are; the good news is that because of Jesus we don't have to.**

# HAVE COURAGE

### Read 1 Corinthians 16:13-14.

*"Be on your guard; stand firm in the faith; be men of courage; be strong" (v. 13).*

Sportswriter Bill Haisten wrote, "Football is a violent game that requires of its participants a certain measure of courage." That's why Clint Coe was able to play it.

A defensive back, Coe completed his eligibility at Oklahoma State in 2007 as a member of the punt coverage, punt return, and kickoff return teams. The story lay not in his being on all three units, but that he was on the field at all.

Coe suffered "a litany of physical setbacks" that should have forced him to give up the game long before he played for State in 2007. But he persisted, leading Cowboy coaches and players to repeatedly express their respect for him.

That "litany of physical setbacks" began in Coe's sophomore season in high school when he missed six games with a hip injury. As a senior, he sustained a concussion. While doctors were treating him, they discovered he had two fractured vertebrae.

During the first week of spring practice at OSU in 2006, he tore a ligament in his left knee. After surgery, he rehabbed all summer and returned in time for preseason practice in August.

Then on Aug. 27, he was the victim of a violent assault. He required surgery to rebuild his lower lip and repair damaged nasal passages. He was expected to miss the whole season. Instead, he returned in time to play in eight games.

So why didn't he just quit football? "I feel like God puts these situations in your life to see how you'll react," he said. "I didn't want to be one of those guys that lays down and takes the easy way out."

No, that would show a lack of courage, something of which Coe has never been accused.

When we speak of courage, we often think of heroic actions such as those displayed by soldiers during wartime or firefighters during an inferno. But as Clint Coe's life demonstrates, there is another aspect to courage.

What makes Coe's life a fit example of courage is not the absence of fear, which usually results from foolhardiness or dearth of relevant information. Rather, his courage showed itself in his determined refusal to let fear debilitate him in the face of a stretch of adversity.

This is the courage God calls upon us to demonstrate in our faith lives. When Paul urged the Christians in Corinth to "be men of courage," he wasn't telling them to rush into burning buildings. He was admonishing them to be strong and sure in their faith.

This courageous attitude is an absolute necessity for American Christians today when our faith is under attack as never before. Our spiritual courage reveals itself in our proclaiming the name of Jesus no matter what forces are arrayed against us.

*By anyone's definition, Clint Coe is courageous and tough.*
*-- Sportswriter Bill Haisten*

**To be courageous for Jesus is to speak his name**
**boldly no matter what tactics Satan uses.**

DAY 67

# FOCAL POINT

**Read Psalm 73.**

*"You destroy all who are unfaithful to you. But as for me,
it is good to be near God" (vv. 27b, 28a).*

From undressed cheerleaders to a band next to their bench, the Cowboys had a tough time focusing on the game they had to play.

Oklahoma State wrapped up its 9-2 regular season in 1988 with a game against Texas Tech in Tokyo. Tech was a tough enough opponent, but the Pokes also had to battle a number of distractions. To even warm up before the game, the coaches had to shoo "a whole ocean of guys with cameras" off the field. Head coach Pat Jones found himself distracted when a distressed referee told him he couldn't find the 30-second clock for the game.

The distractions persisted in the locker room as the team waited for the game to start. A commotion arose, and to his consternation, Jones learned that the Miami Dolphins cheerleaders were in the next room dressing for the game with nothing on the door. "Our guys did what you would expect college males to do," he said, and it wasn't sit around and think about football.

"I was so mad about it that I didn't take a peek," Jones said. He did, however, raise enough Cain that somebody finally "got us some stuff to tape over the door so our players could concentrate on the Red Raiders instead of female anatomy."

The distractions continued during the game when the Grambling band wound up next to the OSU bench. The ear-splitting racket worked in OSU's favor once when the line couldn't hear up-back Garrett Limbrick shout the code word to cancel a fake punt. The center snapped the ball to him, and once he got over his surprise, he ran for a first down.

The Pokes kept their focus long enough to win 45-42.

Living by faith and not by sight is sometimes tough. Like the Cowboys in Tokyo, we quite often find ourselves distracted by what is going on around us. Bewildered, we forget what is most important to us and what really matters in life.

Like the psalmist of old, we look around and see the wicked prosper while the godly suffer; we succumb to despair. If we can't beat 'em, then we may as well join 'em. So we lower our eyes and our vision away from God and turn our feet from the path of righteousness and truth. We lose focus; we lose sight of God. We are then easy prey for the world and its temptations.

It is also easy, however, to regain that focus. We need only consider the ultimate fate of those whom we have momentarily envied and sought perhaps to emulate, those who scoff at God, reject Jesus, and cherish the world's trinkets. Their prosperity is fleeting; its permanence is, as the psalmist says, an illusion that God one day will sweep away.

We who keep our focus on God will be sustained by him in this world and will one day be gathered with him into glory.

*It was tough to set a tone to win a football game with everything going on around us.*
*-- Pat Jones on the distractions in Tokyo*

**Children of the world focus on earthly rewards;**
**children of God focus on heavenly rewards.**

# PROMISES, PROMISES

**Read 2 Corinthians 1:16-20.**

*"No matter how many promises God has made, they are 'Yes' in Christ" (v. 20).*

Prior to the Baylor game of 2006, OSU defensive coordinator Vance Bedford made a promise to his players, something about some clippers and his head. His hair never stood a chance.

On Nov. 11, the Cowboys rolled to their greatest point total ever against a Big 12 opponent in routing the Bears 66-24. The win upped the Pokes to 6-4 for the season, thus ensuring their third bowl trip in the last four seasons.

The Bears weren't really *that* bad; they went into the game 3-3 in the Big 12. They experienced, however, what their head coach described as "a total meltdown."

The blowout began in the second quarter when the Cowboys broke a 3-3 tie with five touchdowns to lead 38-3 at intermission. During the game, tailback Keith Toston scored twice, tight end Brandon Pettigrew caught a pair of touchdown passes, defensive end Darnell Smith rumbled 23 yards with an interception for a score, and safety Donovan Woods took a fumble recovery 57 yards for a touchdown. Both the defensive touchdowns came in the third quarter, upping the lead to 52-3. Fullback John Johnson got a fourth-quarter TD on his first carry of the season.

Just about as much fun for the Cowboy players and coaches as the game was what happened in the locker room right afterwards.

# COWBOYS

It seems Bedford had promised his players he would shave his head if they beat Baylor by at least 18 points. That condition, of course, was taken care of by halftime.

So Bedford arrived in the locker room to find a coterie of Cowboys all gathered to witness the shearing and assistant strength coach Trumain Carroll poised with some clippers. "(Carroll) had the chair. He had the clippers ready to go, and they wasted no time at cutting my hair off," Bedford said.

Promise made. Promise kept.

Like Vance Bedford, the promises you make don't say much about you; the promises you keep tell everything.

The promise to your daughter to be there for her softball game. To your son to help him with his math homework. To your parents to come see them soon. To your spouse to remain faithful until death parts you. And remember what you promised God?

You may carelessly throw promises around, but you can never outpromise God, who is downright profligate with his promises. For instance, he has promised to love you always, to forgive you no matter what you do, and to prepare a place for you with him in Heaven.

And there's more good news in that God operates on this simple premise: Promises made are promises kept. You can rely absolutely on God's promises. The people to whom you make them should be able to rely just as surely on your promises.

*I'm too old to have my head shaved; I'm afraid it might not grow back.*
*-- Vance Bedford*

**God keeps his promises just as those**
**who rely on you expect you to keep yours.**

**PROMISES, PROMISES 137**

DAY 69

# PAIN RELIEF

**Read 2 Corinthians 1:3-7.**

*"Just as the sufferings of Christ flow over into our lives, so also through Christ our comfort overflows" (v. 5).*

**F**or Cowgirl third baseman Mariah Gearhart, pain was a part of her game.

Gearhart is one of OSU's greatest softball players ever. From 2008-2011, she posted a career batting average of .347, sixth in school history. Her .463 on-base percentage is third in the record books. She set school records for stolen bases and runs scored.

Gearhart also set an interesting NCAA record; she was hit by a pitch 98 times in college. She already owned the record before her senior season even started, and she was hit another 29 times.

That record wasn't set because of her slow reflexes. As Gearhart learned the game, her dad, exasperated by players who bailed out on inside pitches, instilled the "free-base" mentality into her game. He would position a pitching machine to throw the ball inside and dare his daughter not to move.

Eventually, she didn't. "Just like working on hitting, we worked on getting hit," she recalled. "We basically worked on taking the instinct to move out of me."

Gearhart never leaned into pitches to get hit; she didn't need to. "I'm on the plate more than most people," she said. "I put my toes on the chalk line, but that's it." "She refuses to move," said OSU coach Rich Wieligman. Thus, in Stillwater, Gearhart took one for

138   DAY 69

the team as no other player in the history of college softball has done before or since.

She paid for her steadfast insistence on standing her ground with pain. "I've had some bruises that lasted a couple weeks," she admitted. "It's always fun to see which ones last the longest." The shots to her calves were less "fun" than others. "I'll notice them the longest," she said.

"It's real awkward to say I take pride in it, but I really do," Gearhart said about her pain-inducing NCAA record.

Since you live on Earth and not in Heaven, you are forced to play with pain as Mariah Gearhart did. Whether it's a car wreck that left you shattered, the end of a relationship that left you battered, or a loved one's death that left you tattered -- pain finds you and challenges you to keep going.

While God's word teaches that you will reap what you sow, life also teaches that pain and hardship are not necessarily the result of personal failure. Pain in fact can be one of the tools God uses to mold your character and change your life.

What are you to do when you are hit full-speed by the awful pain that seems to choke the very will to live out of you? Where is your consolation, your comfort, and your help?

In almighty God, whose love will never fail. When life knocks you to your knees, you are closer to God than ever before.

*The 60 feet going from home to first normally is enough time for the pain to go away for me.*
                                   *-- Mariah Gearhart on getting hit by a pitch*

**When life hits you with pain, you can always
turn to God for comfort, consolation, and hope.**

PAIN RELIEF    139

# PLAN AHEAD

**Read Psalm 33:1-15.**

*"The plans of the Lord stand firm forever, the purposes of his heart through all generations" (v. 11).*

The Cowboys pulled off the "Miracle in the Rockies" because a couple of the coaches had planned ahead.

In Jimmy Johnson's first season in Stillwater, the 1979 football team was still feeling the effects of NCAA probation. Only eight seniors and a total of 62 scholarship players suited up for the first game. A string of injuries rendered the situation so dire that the Cowboys soon had a two-deep roster of which more than half the players were freshmen or walk-ons.

Johnson's defensive boss was Pat Jones, who would succeed him as head coach. Jones said that despite the shortage of bodies, talented or otherwise, "the ball bounced our way that first season partially because we made our own breaks." Some careful planning made just such a break in the Nov. 10 game against Colorado.

The Buffaloes led 20-14 with less than four minutes to play when the Colorado coaches decided to put the game away. Facing fourth down and short yardage at their own 38, they decided to go for it. "If they had punted, we probably weren't going to drive the field and win the game," Jones observed.

The surprise move didn't faze Johnson or Jones one bit because they had talked over what they would do in just such a situation. They had decided to use their goal-line defense no matter what side of the field the ball was on. "If they threw the ball, fine. if they got us, they got us," Jones said.

Colorado ran a quarterback sneak right into the teeth of that goal-line defense. Nose guard Steve Heinzler and Darryl Sheffey were there to stop him short.

With less than two minutes to go, junior quarterback Harold Bailey hit wide receiver Mel Campbell on a play-action pass for a touchdown that lifted the shorthanded Cowboys to 5-4 for the season. Jones called the 21-20 win the "Miracle in the Rockies." It was helped along, though, by some careful planning.

Successful living takes planning. You go to school to improve your chances for a better paying job. You use blueprints to build your home. You plan for retirement. You map out your vacation to have the best time. You even plan your children -- sometimes.

Your best-laid plans, however, sometime get wrecked by events and circumstances beyond your control. The economy goes into the tank; a debilitating illness strikes; a tornado hits. Life is capricious and thus no plans -- not even your best ones -- are foolproof.

But you don't have to go it alone. God has plans for your life that guarantee success as God defines it if you will make him your planning partner. God's plan for your life includes joy, love, peace, kindness, gentleness, and faithfulness, all the elements necessary for truly successful living for today and for all eternity. And God's plan will not fail.

*A man without a plan doesn't have a future.*
*-- TCU head football coach Gary Patterson*

**Your plans may ensure a successful life;**
**God's plans will ensure a successful eternity.**

# THE SUB

**Read Galatians 3:10-14.**

*"Christ redeemed us from the curse of the law by becoming a curse for us" (v. 13).*

After two straight disheartening losses, the last thing the Cowboys needed was for their star tailback to have knee problems. Good thing they had a sub.

OSU was 6-3 and ranked 25th when Baylor came to town on Nov. 13, 2004, but two of those losses had come over the last two weeks. The season was in danger of unraveling, especially when Vernand Morency, the nation's sixth-leading rusher, came up hobbling with a sore knee. Through the nine games, he had averaged 25 carries per contest, and the grind had simply worn him down some. The team turned to backup senior Seymore Shaw.

The Cowboys got him at a good time. A member of Les Miles' first recruiting class, Shaw had battled injuries for three seasons. He broke his foot as a freshman and also battled a broken fibula and numerous twisted ankles over the years. He missed the Cotton Bowl his junior season with a pulled thigh muscle.

But just when his team needed him the most, Shaw was at his healthiest. He "came off the bench in style," lending some gloss to OSU's reputation as Tailback U. Shaw rushed for 172 yards on 30 carries, both career highs. He led a Cowboy running attack that gobbled up 305 yards, the second-highest rushing total of the season. When the dust from all that ground game cleared, State had a 49-21 blowout on its hands.

The dominance of the Cowboy ground game was illustrated most strikingly in the second quarter when State ground out an 18-play, 88-yard drive that ate nine minutes off the clock. Fittingly, Shaw put on the finishing touch with a 15-yard touchdown run.

"They just mashed us up front," said the Baylor head coach. The head masher was Shaw, the sub who stepped up.

Wouldn't it be cool if you had a substitute like Seymore Shaw for all life's hard stuff? Telling of a death in the family? Call in your sub. Breaking up with your boyfriend? Job interview? Chemistry test? Crucial presentation at work? Let the sub handle it.

We do have such a substitute, but not for the matters of life. Instead, Jesus is our substitute for matters of life and death. Since Jesus has already made it, we don't have to make the sacrifice God demands for forgiveness and salvation.

One of the most pathetic aspects of our contemporary times is that many people deny Jesus Christ and then desperately cast about for a substitute for him. Mysticism, human philosophies such as Scientology, false religions such as Hinduism and Islam, cults, New Age approaches that preach self-fulfillment without responsibility or accountability – they and others like them are all pitiful, inadequate substitutes for Jesus.

There is no substitute for Jesus. It's Jesus or nothing.

*I never substitute just to substitute. The only way a guy gets off the floor is if he dies.*

-- *Former basketball coach Abe Lemons*

**There is no substitute for Jesus,
the consummate sub.**

DAY 72

# STORY TIME

**Read Luke 8:26-39.**

*"'Return home and tell how much God has done for you.'*
*So the man went away and told all over town how much*
*Jesus had done for him" (v. 39).*

From a couple frozen to their seats to an unusual chore in the press box to a coach's threat not to play the game -- stories swirled around the 1985 version of Bedlam, the legendary "Ice Bowl."

For only the second time in the series' 93-game history, the 1985 Bedlam was a night game, with kickoff at 6 p.m. Athletic Director Myron Roderick moved the game to the evening to accommodate television, which would help pay for $750,000 worth of new lights that had recently been installed at Lewis Field. OU head coach Barry Switzer didn't like it one bit, even threatening not to show up. "He was throwing his weight around a little," Roderick said.

Switzer wasn't the only one complaining, though, when game time arrived. The rain started innocently enough, but when the temperature dropped, the rain turned to sleet and the field turned into a hockey rink. As Roderick put it, "It could have been a nice evening, but it didn't turn out that way."

Steve Buzzard, later the OSU media relations director, had one rather onerous chore that long, cold night: to keep the press box window free of condensation. "I never caught up with the job, though. It was awful," he said.

Switzer complained after the game that his right foot "was so cold and hurt so much that I was afraid I had frostbite." His problem was nothing, however, compared to that of a pair of Cowboy fans. Dr. Donald Cooper, who was then the OSU team physician, told the story of a couple who were still in their seats after the stadium had quickly cleared. When the police asked them why they were still there, they were told "the gal had wet her pants and froze them to the aluminum seats." According to Cooper, "workers freed the human popsicles by retrieving hot coffee from a vendor and pouring it down her backside."

So you don't have any story to relate from the 1985 Ice Bowl. You nevertheless have a story to tell; it's the story of your life and it's unique. No one else among the billions of people on this planet can tell the same story.

Part of that story is your encounter with Jesus. It's the most important chapter of all, but, strangely enough, believers in Jesus Christ often don't tell it. Otherwise brave and daring Christian men and women who wouldn't think twice of skydiving or whitewater rafting often quail when they are faced with the prospect of speaking about Jesus to someone else. It's the dreaded "W" word: witness. "I just don't know what to say," they sputter.

But witnessing is nothing but telling your story. No one can refute it; no one can claim it isn't true. You don't get into some great theological debate for which you're ill prepared. You just tell the beautiful, awesome story of Jesus and you.

*That's the way it happened. It's pretty unusual.*
*-- Dr. Donald Cooper and his story about the frozen fans*

**We all have a story to tell, but the most important part of all is the chapter where we meet Jesus.**

# CELEBRATION TIME

**Read Luke 15:1-10.**

*"There is rejoicing in the presence of the angels of God over one sinner who repents" (v. 10).*

A roar, a cartwheel and a back flip, a deep breath. They were ways the Cowboys found to celebrate after they pulled off a feat that hadn't been accomplished in 55 years.

On Feb. 2, 2013, the 15-5 OSU men's basketball team went on the road and upset second-ranked Kansas 85-80. The win ended the Jayhawks' 18-game winning streak -- tops in the country. The victory marked the first time since a defeat of Kansas in 1958 that the Cowboys beat a top-5 team on the road.

To grab the win, the Pokes had to show what they were made of. They jumped out to a 14-point lead in the first half, but the Jayhawks didn't notch that long win streak by quitting when they fell behind. They rallied and pulled out to a six-point lead with less than five minutes to play. But, "in one of the rare instances of a team refusing to lose at intimidating Allen Fieldhouse, [Markel] Brown and [Marcus] Smart managed to hold things together."

Brown, a junior forward who was Second Team All-Big 12, led all Cowboy scorers with 28 points. Smart scored seven of his 25 points in the game's final minutes. A guard, Smart had a specta-cular freshman season. He won the Integris Wayman Tisdale Award, presented annually by the U.S. Basketball Writers Association to the nation's top freshman. *Sporting News* named him a first-team All-America and its national Freshman of the Year. He was unanimously selected as the Big 12 Player of the Year and the Big 12 Freshman of the Year, and he was a unanimous choice for the All-Big 12 First Team.

When the game ended, the celebration began. Brown let out a roar, and head coach Travis Ford exhaled "for the first time all game." Smart topped them all, launching into a cartwheel and back flip combination on the court.

State just whipped Oklahoma. You got that new job or that promotion. You just held your newborn child in your arms. Life has those grand moments that call for celebration. You may jump up and down and scream in a wild frenzy at an OSU game or share a sedate candlelight dinner at home -- but you celebrate.

Consider then a celebration that is beyond our imagining, one that fills every corner of the home of God and the angels. Imagine a celebration in Heaven, which also has its grand moments.

Those grand moments are touched off when someone comes to faith in Jesus. Heaven itself rings with the joyous sounds of the singing and dancing of the celebrating angels. Even God rejoices when just one person – you or someone you have introduced to Christ -- turns to him.

When you said "yes" to Christ, you made the angels dance. Most importantly of all, you made God smile.

*I was so ecstatic about the victory it just came to me to do it.*
*-- Marcus Smart on his celebratory gymnastics*

**God himself joins the angels in heavenly celebration when even a single person turns to him through faith in Jesus.**

# PRACTICE SESSION

**Read 2 Peter 1:3-11.**

*"For if you do these things, you will never fail, and you
will receive a rich welcome into the eternal kingdom of our
Lord and Savior Jesus Christ" (vv. 10b-11).*

**P**ractice certainly didn't make the Cowboys perfect, but it did
enable them to pull out a last-gasp win over Kansas State.

On Oct. 20, 2007, State and the 25th-ranked Wildcats put on a
wild and woolly shootout in Stillwater. The most exciting play
of the first half was delivered by cornerback Perrish Cox, who
returned a Cat kickoff 98 yards for a touchdown.

But then came a heartpounding fourth quarter when the two
teams combined for 28 points. The Cats seemed to have saved
themselves when they scored with 1:11 to play and then disdained
the tie with a two-point conversion for a 39-38 lead.

The Cowboys, however, were unperturbed because the tough
situation they now faced was familiar to them. "We go through
these scenarios all the time," said offensive coordinator Larry
Fedora. So what the offense faced was no different from what they
practiced every Wednesday. The practice paid off.

Tommy Devereaux set the offense up with a 26-yard kickoff
return to the State 42. That gave the Pokes enough field position
to run the ball, which they did. Quarterback Zac Robinson went
for 14, and tailback Dantrell Savage got 7 yards. Robinson then
lofted a 24-yard pass down the sideline to Savage for the drive's

only pass. Savage wound up at the Cat 18 with 38 seconds left. Interestingly, that pass play was one the State offense hadn't practiced during their last-minute drills. "I don't think he's used to making that catch," Robinson said of his tailback's clutch grab. With six seconds left, Jason Ricks completed the drill with a 26-yard field goal. Just like practice. Only this time, the Cowboys had a for-real 41-39 win.

Imagine a football team that never practices. A play cast that doesn't rehearse. A preacher who never reviews or practices his sermon beforehand. When the showdown comes, they would be revealed as inept bumblers that merit our disdain.

We practice something so that we will become good at it, so that it becomes so natural that we can pull it off without even having to think about it. Interestingly, if we are to live as Christ wants us to, then we must practice that lifestyle — and showing up at church and sitting stoically on a pew once a week does not constitute practice. To practice successfully, we must participate; we must do repeatedly whatever it is we want to be good at.

We must practice being like Christ by living like Christ every day of our lives. For Christians, practice is a lifestyle that doesn't make perfect -- only Christ is perfect — but it does prepare us for the real thing: the day we meet God face to face and inherit Christ's kingdom.

*There's [no] doubt these kids have confidence in that situation.*
*-- Larry Fedora on the result of practicing last-minute drives*

**Practicing the Christian lifestyle doesn't
make us perfect, but it does secure us
a permanent place beside the perfect one.**

# RUN FOR IT

**Read John 20:1-10.**

*"Peter and the other disciple started for the tomb. Both were running, but the other disciple outran Peter and reached the tomb first" (vv. 3-4).*

**M**ike Yurcich outran his wife once, and that's good enough for him. It probably has to be.

Oklahoma State head coach Mike Gundy surprised virtually everyone prior to the 2013 season when he hired Yurcich as his offensive coordinator. The astonishment came about because the boss Poke plucked Yurcich out of Shippensburg University, a Division II school in Pennsylvania.

Following his days as a quarterback at California University in Pennsylvania, also a Division II school, Yurcich made the move into coaching and wound up at Edinboro University, yet another Division II school in the Keystone State. There he met Julie Nemergut, an All-American cross country and track and field athlete who was coaching after having exhausted her eligibility. Her sights were set on a post-college running career, so she wasn't looking for a boyfriend. She went on the first date -- for which Mike was 30 minutes late -- and had no interest in a second one. A roommate persuaded her to go -- to an arena football game.

After they married and both continued their coaching careers at Edinboro, Mike turned down opportunities to move up. Julie's response was to quit, leaving him free to look for a bigger job.

Two days later, he was hired at Shippensburg. The rest is history. The competitive pair even go hard at it against each other in Wiffle Ball, but Mike could never outun her. Except once. After the pregnancy of one of their sons, Julie was headed for a run and Mike said he wanted to come along. She knew what he was up to, and he outpaced her that day.

That was the last time, though; she has outrun him ever since. "I got that one," he said in response to a dig about not being able to keep up with his wife. "That's all I will say there."

Hit the ground running -- every morning that's what you do as you leave the house and re-enter the rat race. You run errands; you run though a presentation; you give someone a run for his money; you always want to be in the running and never run-of-the-mill.

You're always running toward something, such as your goals, or away from something, such as your past. Many of us spend much of our lives foolishly attempting to run away from God, the purposes he has for us, and the blessings he is waiting to give us.

No matter how hard or how far you run, though, you can never outrun yourself or God. God keeps pace with you, calling you in the short run to take care of the long run by falling to your knees and running for your life -- to Jesus -- just as Peter and the other disciple ran that first Easter morning.

On your knees, you run all the way to glory.

*From his first step, I knew what his intentions were. It wasn't like, 'Let's go for a nice jog and spend time together.'*
        *-- Julie Yurcich on the one day hubby Mike outran her*

**You can run to eternity by going to your knees.**

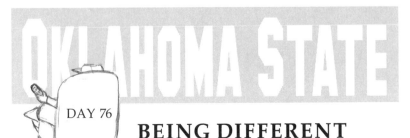

# BEING DIFFERENT

### Read Daniel 3.

*"We want you to know, O king, that we will not serve your gods or worship the image of gold you have set up" (v. 18).*

**F**rom a roped-off ring to full-length wool tights -- wrestling at Oklahoma State was once quite different from what it is now.

In the 1920s and '30s, the Cowboys had only a few dual meets each season, unlike today's packed schedule. Five to eight meets constituted a full slate.

What the Cowboys wore at one time was also quite different from today's outfits. Through much of the 1920s during the Ed Gallagher years (1916-1940), they wore full-length wool tights. In the late 1930s, the move was made to wool trunks with no tights.

The team also used to wrestle bare-chested at home meets (outlawed by the NCAA in the 1960s). When they went east, however, the host schools often requested that they put on sleeveless shirts. Missing also was headgear, rare in the Gallagher era.

At one time, the Cowboys wrestled at home in a roped-off ring (banned by the NCAA in the early 1940s). Though the official rule book of the day provided extensive details about the size of the rings, the number of the ropes, and what the ropes were to be made of, it was silent on how the ropes could be used. During one match, an apparently quite irritated Cowboy wrestler tossed his opponent over the top rope and out of the ring. He wasn't

# COWBOYS

disqualified and the match resumed once the now-reluctant loyal opposition made his way back into the ring.

No matter when we're talking about, one thing was not a bit different from today's OSU wrestling program: winning. A Cowboy wrestler in wool tights who climbed into a roped-off ring would certainly be different and would stand out today. In many ways, Christians are called to stand out like that.

That's because while we live in a secular society that constantly pressures us to conform to its principles and its values, we serve a risen Christ who calls us to be different. Therein lies the great conflict of the Christian life in contemporary America.

But how many of us really consider that even in our secular society we struggle to conform? We are all geeks in a sense. We can never truly conform because we were not created by God to live in such a sin-filled world in the first place. Thus, when Christ calls us to be different by following and espousing Christian beliefs, principles, and practices, he is summoning us to the lifestyle we were born for.

The most important step in being different for Jesus is realizing and admitting what we really are: We are children of God; we are Christians. Only secondarily are we citizens of a secular world. That world both scorns and disdains us for being different; Jesus both praises and loves us for it.

*Outfitted in Stetson hats, colorful flannel shirts, and cowboy boots, team members made an incredible impression whenever they traveled.*
*-- Mark Palmer on a different type of road dress for OSU wrestlers*

**The lifestyle Jesus calls us to is different from that of the world, but it is the way we were born to live.**

# TEN TO REMEMBER

### Read Exodus 20:1-17.

*"God spoke all these words: 'I am the Lord your God . . . .*
*You shall have no other gods before me'" (vv. 1, 3).*

**F**rom Zac Robinson to Barry Sanders, Athlon Sports has ranked the ten greatest Oklahoma State football players since 1967.

Robinson, No. 10 on the list, was the school's all-time leader in total offense before his senior season. From 2007-09, he threw for 10,175 yards and a school-record 66 touchdowns.

Athlon's No. 9 was quarterback Brandon Weeden. In 2010 and 2011, he led the Pokes to two of their most storied seasons (11-2 and 12-1). He owns the school single-season records for passing yards (4,727) and passing touchdowns (37), among others.

Defensive end Jason Gildon (1990-93) was ranked No. 8 on the ten greatest list. His 35.5 career sacks are still the school record.

No. 7 on the list was running back Terry Miller (1974-77). The two-time All-America rushed for 4,581 yards, which still leaves him second all-time in school history.

Wide receiver Justin Blackmon (2009-11) was Athlon's sixth-greatest OSU player. He was a two-time All-America and twice won the Fred Biletnikoff Award as the nation's best receiver. He "is arguably the most productive receiver in program history."

No. 5 on the top-ten list is wide receiver Rashaun Woods (2000-03). He set many school records that Blackmon subsequently broke. Fourth on the list is offensive tackle Russell Okung (2006-

09), a consensus All-America and the Big 12 Offensive Lineman of the Year in 2009. Named by Athlon as No. 3 was defensive lineman Leslie O'Neal (1982-85), the league's Defensive Player of the Year in 1984 and three times all-conference.

A pair of legendary running backs tops the list. No. 2 is Thurman Thomas (1984-87), State's all-time leading rusher with 4,595 yards. And Athlon's all-time greatest Cowboy player since 1967 is Barry Sanders, the 1988 Heisman Trophy winner.

For OSU fans, these are indeed ten to remember for the ages.

You've got your list and you're ready to go: a gallon of paint and a water hose from the hardware store; chips, peanuts, and sodas from the grocery store for watching tonight's football game with your buddies; the tickets for the band concert. Your list helps you remember.

God also made a list once of things he wanted you to remember; it's called the Ten Commandments. Just as your list reminds you to do something, so does God's list remind you of how you are to act in your dealings with other people and with him. A life dedicated to Jesus is a life devoted to relationships, and God's list emphasizes that the social life and the spiritual life of the faithful cannot be sundered. God's relationship to you is one of unceasing, unqualified love, and you are to mirror that divine love in your relationships with others. In case you forget, you have a list.

*Society today treats the Ten Commandments as if they were the ten suggestions. Never compromise on right or wrong.*
*-- College baseball coach Gordie Gillespie*

**God's list is a set of instructions on how you are to conduct yourself with other people and with him.**

# WHO CARES?

**Read Revelation 3:14-20.**

*"[B]ecause you are lukewarm – neither hot nor bold – I am about to spit you out of my mouth" (v. 16).*

**B**arry Hanna was totally indifferent to what his coaches were screaming at him to do. The result was a game-winning touchdown.

In 1984, the Cowboys went 9-2 and finished the regular season ranked No. 9. They accepted a bid to play 10-1 and seventh-ranked South Carolina in the Gator Bowl on Dec. 28. It was a thriller.

OSU scored the game's first thirteen points. The second touchdown came on a little bit of razzle-dazzle from the Gamecock 6. Quarterback Rusty Hilger pitched to tailback Thurman Thomas, who swept right, suddenly drew up short, and lofted a TD pass to a wide open Hilger. The PAT was wide, though, which set up an exciting finish.

South Carolina rallied to lead 14-13 well into the last quarter. OSU got the ball on its own 12 for what everyone knew would be the Pokes' last chance to win it. "We started dinking and dunking," head coach Pat Jones said. With the Pokes down to their last shot on a fourth-and-six, Hilger found Hanna, his senior tight end. He chugged for a first down at the USC 36. Thomas then got 11 yards on a draw, and OSU was in field goal range.

With more than a minute and a half left to play, Jones decided to get closer, and Hilger hit the ever-reliable Hanna on a crossing route. The coaches right away started screaming for him to get out of bounds and stop the clock. Instead, Hanna "brutally drove [the ball] into the end zone." He flattened two defenders and crossed the goal line with two more Gamecocks hanging on and 94 seconds on the clock. Hanna's indifference and determination earned OSU a 21-14 win and the school's first-ever 10-win season. It was his only touchdown catch of the season.

Too many of us can sum up our attitude about ignorance and indifference pretty simply: "I don't know and I don't care." Our generally pitiful turnouts for national and state elections are an example of our national indifference, even about some aspects of life that ought to matter greatly to us.

Our disregard for much that is superfluous in our lives does us no harm. When our indifference seeps insidiously into our faith life, though, we are placing our immortal souls in danger.

Too many modern-day followers of Jesus Christ are indifferent Christians. They go through the motions of showing up for church or a fellowship meal. They do not, however, allow God to make a difference in their lives. It's not that they don't care about God at all; they just don't care enough. They are lukewarm.

Jesus made it very clear what the result of that indifference would be with the terrifying declaration, "I am about to spit you out of my mouth." No matter what we may say about Jesus, we can never say he is indifferent, not even to the least of us.

*The trouble with referees is they just don't care which side wins.*
-- Writer Tom Canterbury

**Indifference didn't drive Jesus to that cross, and indifference to that cross won't save us.**

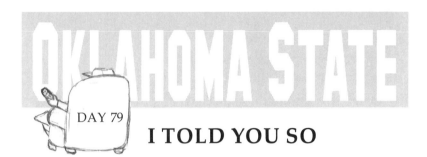

# I TOLD YOU SO

**Read Matthew 24:15-31.**

*"See, I have told you ahead of time" (v. 25).*

After a game in which he made one of the biggest plays of the 2011 season, State defensive end Richetti Jones put on his "I-told-you-so" face -- but it didn't have anything to do with the win.

On the final play of the Kansas State game, Jones pressured the Wildcat quarterback into a bad throw that preserved an exciting 52-45 OSU win and kept the Cowboys undefeated. (See Devotion No. 43.) Jones was such a charismatic leader and speaker that the coaches often pressed him into duty to host recruits on campus.

He had a definite opinion about that game-ending defensive stand against K State. The Cats ran a play from the State 5 with five seconds left, and Brodrick Brown batted a pass away in the end zone. "I am like, 'yes, it's over,'" Jones said. To his surprise and contempt, the clock still showed one second. "We are at home and they left one second on the clock. Really?" he said. "That's something that happens when you are on the road."

Jones also could colorfully describe his first encounter with an Oklahoma earthquake, "I woke up and my lamp was making like a jiggling noise. I was like, '. . . paranormal activity is in my room right now.' And I started praying and I just went back to sleep. But I felt much better when I found out it was an earthquake."

After Jones' play against K State, pandemonium broke loose in Boone Pickens Stadium. When the stadium began to tremble, some of the Cowboys attributed the shaking to the boisterous and exuberant home crowd. Not Jones.

"Coach Gundy, he is just sitting there talking and giving his speech and I didn't want to be rude or too loud," Jones said, "so I just put it out there (quietly that) it's an earthquake." His teammates had nothing but disdain for Jones' assertion, but when he saw the news on TV later, he made sure he told them so. The tremors had indeed resulted from an earthquake.

Don't you just hate it in when somebody says, "I told you so"? That means the other person was right and you were wrong; that other person has spoken the truth. You could have listened to that know-it-all in the first place, but then you would have lost the chance yourself to crow, "I told you so."

In our pluralistic age and society, many view truth as relative, meaning absolute truth does not exist. All belief systems have equal value and merit. But this is a ghastly, dangerous fallacy because it ignores the truth that God proclaimed in the presence and words of Jesus.

In speaking the truth, Jesus told everybody exactly what he was going to do: come back and take his faithful followers with him. Those who don't listen or who don't believe will be left behind with those four awful words, "I told you so," ringing in their ears and wringing their souls.

*When I got home and saw that [an earthquake] was on the news, I came back with an I-told-you-so face.*
*-- Richetti Jones after the 2011 K-State game*

**Jesus matter-of-factly told us what he has planned:**
**He will return to gather all the faithful to himself.**

# HANGING IN THERE

### Read Mark 14:32-42.

*"'Father,' he said, 'everything is possible for you. Take this cup from me. Yet not what I will, but what you will'" (v. 36).*

**D**octors told Megan Byford the pain in her knees would be too much for her if she tried to play basketball again. They had no idea how persistent she was.

Four surgeries in seven years meant that Byford's knees were a mess. Her doctors said her knees were so damaged she should forget about basketball. "I'm sure doctors have all said if it had been anyone else, there is no way they could play through it with the kind of knees that I have," Byford said.

But she recounted the doctors' opinions in 2010 as she neared the end of her third and final season as an OSU basketball player. Byford simply persisted, playing through the pain with the help of a pair of knee braces, ice packs, and a daily strengthening and conditioning regimen.

The pain in her knees wasn't just on the court either. She started every morning with stiff knees. They ached when the weather turned cold. She couldn't water ski or do anything that put pressure on her knees. "Car rides aren't fun," she said. "Having to be folded up in a car seat for a long time, they get stiff."

Her head coach, the late Kurt Budke, said the staff hoped for about ten minutes a game off the bench from Byford. Instead, "she willed herself into becoming good enough to become an effective starter in the Big 12."

She lettered three times and finished her career fourth all-time in field-goal percentage and sixth all-time in blocked shots. Love and persistence drove her. "I love basketball," Byford said. "I'm stubborn and I've always wanted to prove people wrong." Faith made it possible. "I know God has blessed me with the ability to ignore the pain," she said, "so he's really been good to me."

And so Megan Byford persisted in spite of the pain.

Life is tough; it inevitably beats us up and kicks us around some. But life has four quarters, and so here we are, still standing, still in the game. We know that we can never win if we don't finish. We emerge as winners and champions only if we never give up, if we just see it through as Megan Byford did at OSU.

Interestingly, Jesus has been in the same situation. On that awful night in the garden, Jesus understood the nature of the suffering he was about to undergo, and he begged God to take it from him. In the end, though, he yielded to God's will and surrendered his own.

Even in the matter of persistence, Jesus is our example. As he did, we push doggedly and determinedly ahead – following God's will for our lives -- no matter how hard it gets. And we can do it because God is with us.

*For what she can give with those knees, I promise she's outworking everybody every single day on [the] floor.*
*— The late Kurt Budke on Megan Byford*

**It's tough to keep going, but you have the power of almighty God to pull you through.**

# ANIMAL MAGNETISM

### Read Psalm 139:1-18.

*"For you created my inmost being; you knit me together in my mother's womb. I praise you because I am fearfully and wonderfully made" (vv. 13-14).*

**A**ny experienced football fan knows to prepare sometimes for rain on game day. But a deluge of crickets?

The Cowboys bombed Texas Tech 41-21 on Oct. 9, 1999, at Lewis Field. Sophomore quarterback B.J. Tiger threw for 203 yards that including two TDs and rushed for another score. The game was a bit unusual in that only one week after OSU ran the ball on 18 of its first 20 plays against Nebraska, the Cowboys came out of the chute with some offensive hijinks. OSU drove for touchdowns on its first two possessions using two reverses, two fake reverses, and a fourth-and-1 gamble. The Cowboys also got an unusual scoring pass in the second quarter from fullback Kevin Brown. Tight end Marcellus Rivers was the intended receiver, but a Tech safety deflected the ball right into Brown's hands.

Nothing in the night game, though, was nearly as strange as what happened right after it ended. Suddenly "millions of crickets rained down on the crowd in a phenomenon of Biblical proportion." Shannon Porter, an OSU Alumni Association secretary, said the varmints "were everywhere and falling down on everybody." Another association worker said simply, "It was creepy."

With crickets falling like rain though the skies were cloudless, some Cowboy fans returned to their cars with their umbrellas up, crunching crickets under their feet all the while. The insects were so numerous they covered light poles and ticket offices. Even on Tuesday, some sections outside the stadium had live crickets.

An extension entomologist said the outbreak was a natural result of the state's hot, dry summer and little could be done to control them. He noted they would not be much of a nuisance at the next game, which started at 11:30 a.m.

Many animals elicit our awe and our respect, though crickets and similar insects generally draw a different response. Nothing enlivens a trip more than glimpsing animals in the wild. Admit it: You go along with the kids' trip to the zoo because you think it's a cool place too. All that variety of life is mind-boggling. Who could conceive of a cricket, a walrus, a moose, or a prairie dog? Who could possibly have that rich an imagination?

But the next time you're in a crowd, look around at the parade of faces. Who could come up with the idea for all those different people? For that matter, who could conceive of you? You are unique, a masterpiece who will never be duplicated.

The master creator, God Almighty, is behind it all. He thought of you and brought you into being. If you had a manufacturer's label, it might say, "Lovingly, fearfully, and wonderfully handmade in Heaven by #1 -- God."

*We were picking them off each other and throwing them out the (press box) window.*
*OSU radio broadcaster Bill Teegins on the great cricket invasion of '99*

**You may consider a painting or an animal
a work of art, but the real masterpiece is you.**

# HERO WORSHIP

### Read 1 Samuel 16:1-13.

*"Do not consider his appearance or his height, for . . . the Lord does not look at the things man looks at. . . . The Lord looks at the heart" (v. 7).*

The Cowboys desperately needed a hero to step up -- anybody to do anything -- to avoid a meltdown of legendary proportions.

Texas Tech head coach Mike Leach brought his "basketball-on-grass" offense to Stillwater on Oct. 18, 2003, and what resulted was perhaps the most nerve-racking game Cowboy fans had ever witnessed. Behind tailback Tatum Bell's career-high 238 yards and three touchdowns, State sat comfortably in front 48-21 in the fourth quarter. Game over. Or maybe not.

Tech suddenly cranked its offense up, moving 95 yards quickly, then recovering an onside kick and scoring again. 48-35 and the lead wasn't comfortable anymore. When State was forced into its only punt of the game, that basketball offense struck again, going 84 yards to score. With 9:09 on the clock, State led only 48-42.

The Cowboys stopped the bleeding long enough to drive 68 yards and get a Luke Phillips field goal with 5:43 left. 51-42. But the relentless Tech offense broke loose again, going 80 yards in 1:52. The Red Raiders had outscored State 28-3 in the fourth quarter and trailed only 51-49.

State had to keep the ball away from that offense, but a fourth-down gamble failed to pick up a first down. The machine that had mauled the Cowboys in a frenzied fourth quarter had the ball again with 2:09 left. The first Raider play went for 20 yards. Times were desperate. Somebody had to step up and be a hero.

Two somebodies did. First, senior end Antonio Smith sacked the Tech quarterback for a 15-yard loss. Then safety Jon Holland snared an interception with 1:05 left. Two heroes had saved the Cowboys and their 51-49 win.

For an athlete, a hero is somebody who makes big or clutch plays key to a win. In other fields, a hero is commonly thought of as someone who performs brave and dangerous feats that save or protect someone's life. You figure that excludes you.

But ask your son about that when you show him how to bait a hook or throw a football, or your daughter when you show up for her honors night at school. Look into the eyes of those Little Leaguers you help coach.

Ask God about heroism when you're steady in your faith. For God, a hero is a person with the heart of a servant. And if a hero is a servant who acts to save other's lives, then the greatest hero of all is Jesus Christ.

God seeks heroes today, those who will proclaim the name of their hero – Jesus – proudly and boldly, no matter how others may scoff or ridicule. God knows heroes when he sees them -- by what's in their hearts.

*Right before I went out there [for the last Texas Tech drive] I had my head between my knees thinking I had to make a play.*
*-- Antonio Smith, who indeed made a play*

**God's heroes are those who remain steady
in their faith while serving others.**

# ON CALL

**Read 1 Samuel 3:1-18.**

*"The Lord came and stood there, calling as at the other times, 'Samuel! Samuel!' Then Samuel said, 'Speak, for your servant is listening'" (v. 10).*

Taylor Sokolosky heard the call. When he answered it, he became one of the unlikeliest Oklahoma State football players ever.

Tennis was Sokolosky's game in high school, and he was very good at it, winning four straight championships. "I played some flag football when I was, probably, 10," he recalled. But his senior year, he decided to play football simply because all of his friends were on the team. He was pretty good at that, too. Playing wide receiver, he scored twelve touchdowns for a state runner-up and was the district Receiver of the Year.

It turned out Sokolosky had found a calling; he loved playing football and he wanted to play some more. Neither his resume nor his size impressed anyone, however. He stood 5-foot-9 and weighed 190 pounds. And he had played just one season at "an elite private school known more for its country club sports."

A lifelong Cowboys fan, Sokolosky decided to walk on in Stillwater in 2007. One of his coaches suggested the only way he could ever get on the field was to concentrate on special teams.

It took the freshman one special teams drill to get noticed. The team was practicing kickoff returns, and he kept racing downfield and blowing up the return. "Why aren't we playing that guy?" one coach asked. Special teams coordinator Joe DeForest answered the question by striding over to Sokolosky and saying, "Congratulations. You just made the starting kickoff coverage team."

In 2007 and 2008, this unlikely player who answered the call his heart placed on him made tackles on kickoff coverage and key blocks on big returns and was the holder on field goal and extra point tries. Sokolosky's playing days ended with a broken neck suffered on Oct. 17, 2009, against Missouri. Rather than risk paralysis, he walked away from the game.

A team player is someone who does whatever the coach calls upon him to do for the good of the team as Taylor Sokolosky did. Something quite similar occurs when God places a specific call upon a Christian's life.

For many Christians, though, the idea of answering God's call is scary. That's because many folks understand it to mean going into the ministry, packing the family up, and moving halfway around the world to some place where folks have never heard of air conditioning, fried chicken, paved roads, or the Oklahoma State Cowboys. Zambia. The Philippines. Cleveland even.

Not for you, no thank you. And who can blame you?

But God usually calls folks to serve him where they are. In fact, God put you where you are right now, and he has a purpose in placing you there. Wherever you are, you are called to serve him.

*I didn't feel I got quite all that I wanted to get out of it. I wanted to come to college [and] keep playing.*
       *-- Taylor Sokolosky on answering the call to play college ball*

**God calls you to serve him right now
right where he has put you, wherever that is.**

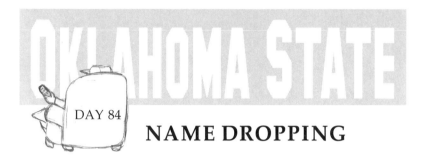

DAY 84

# NAME DROPPING

**Read Exodus 3:13-20.**

*"God said to Moses, 'I AM WHO I AM. This is what you are to say to the Israelites: 'I AM has sent me to you'"* (v. 14).

**O**klahoma State head coach Eddie Sutton was concerned that Bryant Reeves' family would be offended at the nickname a teammate had slapped upon him. He needn't have worried.

Reeves is an OSU legend. He played for the Cowboys from 1992-95 and finished his career second in school history in scoring and rebounds, third in blocked shots, and first in field goal percentage and field goals made. He was three times All-Big Eight, twice the conference Player of the Year, and twice an All-American. He was inducted into the Oklahoma State Hall of Honor in 2000.

Reeves came to Stillwater from Gans, Okla., population 346 at the time, and he stood 7 feet tall and weighed in at 288 pounds. In a pickup game before Reeves' freshman season, a State player nicknamed him "Big Country." The moniker became so well known and so popular that even on the road in the Big Eight, a player checking in to give Reeves a breather would tell the scorer's table simply, "In for Country."

Early on, Sutton feared that the Reeves clan would take offense at the nickname. So he approached them at a game to talk about it, but never made it. He stopped short when he saw a little old lady with a T-shirt that read, "I'm Country's Grandmother."

Strength coach Leroy Youster shared Sutton's concern until he saw the return address on an envelope in which Reeves' mother had sent her son some pictures. It read "Mama Country."

Reeves' father, Carl, briefly considered the possibility that his son might not like the nickname. So he told him, "You *are* big, and you *are* from the country. What's the shame in either?"

Nicknames such as "Big Country" are not slapped haphazardly upon individuals but rather reflect widely held perceptions about the person named. Proper names can also have a particular physical or character trait associated with them..

Nowhere throughout history has this concept been more prevalent than in the Bible, where a name is not a mere label but is an expression of the essential nature of the named one. That is, a person's name reveals his or her character. Even God shares this concept; to know the name of God is to know God as he has chosen to reveal himself to us.

What does your name say about you? Honest, trustworthy, a seeker of the truth and a person of God? Or does the mention of your name cause your coworkers to whisper snide remarks, your neighbors to roll their eyes, or your friends to start making allowances for you?

Most importantly, what does your name say about you to God? He, too, knows you by name.

*I like the name. It fits.*

-- *Bryant Reeves on his "Big Country" nickname*

**Live so that your name evokes
positive associations from people you know,
from the public, and from God.**

# GOOD ADVICE

**Read Isaiah 8:11-9:7.**

*"And he will be called Wonderful Counselor" (v. 9:6b).*

Pat Jones didn't turn to an agent, an attorney, or anyone employed by the school for advice on how to land the head football coach's job at OSU. He went to The Man.

After the 1983 season, State head coach Jimmy Johnson entered discussions and negotiations with the University of Miami. He called a staff meeting to tell his assistant coaches what was going on. Jones, the team's assistant coach, knew immediately he wanted to pursue the OSU opening. After the meeting, he told Johnson to let him know if anything was about to happen. Johnson suggested that he begin working on getting the job. "I knew then that wheels were in motion," Jones said.

They were. Johnson subsequently called Jones and told him to come over to his house. While he was there, the phone rang; it was Miami's athletic director. The deal was done.

Jones left and went directly to Henry Iba's house for advice, striding right onto the porch and knocking on the door. He wasn't sure how much the Oklahoma State legend could help him in his quest, "but I trusted him."

Iba had some twofold advice for Jones: "don't try to get the job through the media and let your friends get the job for you." He then told Jones not to do anything until he contacted him and went to work wielding his enormous clout.

Iba's advice turned out to be right on the money. Jones later talked for about five minutes with the chairman of the board of regents over dinner at a Holiday Inn. That evening, athletic director Myron Roderick called with one question: "Do you want to be the head coach?" Jones answered, "Yes, sir." The job was his.

Like Pat Jones, we all need a little advice now and then. More often than not, we turn to professional counselors, who are all over the place. Marriage counselors, grief counselors, guidance counselors in our schools, rehabilitation counselors, all sorts of mental health and addiction counselors -- We even have pet counselors. No matter what our situation or problem, we can find plenty of advice for the taking.

The problem, of course, is that we find advice easy to offer but hard to swallow. We also have a rueful tendency to solicit the wrong source for advice, seeking counsel that doesn't really solve our problem but that instead enables us to continue with it.

Our need for outside advice, for an independent perspective on our situation, is actually God-given. God serves many functions in our lives, but one role clearly delineated in his Word is that of Counselor. Jesus himself is described as the "Wonderful Counselor." All the advice we need in our lives is right there for the asking; we don't even have to pay for it except with our faith. God is always there for us: to listen, to lead, and to guide.

*Of every living being on the planet, Mr. Iba was Oklahoma State.*
*-- Pat Jones on why he went to Henry Iba for advice*

**We all need and seek advice in our lives,**
**but the ultimate and most wonderful Counselor**
**is of divine and not human origin.**

# UNEXPECTEDLY

**Read Matthew 24:36-51.**

*"No one knows about that day or hour, not even the angels in heaven, nor the Son, but only the Father" (v. 36).*

**B**randon Weeden had such low expectations of playing that he had to go find his helmet. No one expected that he would come out and save his team from a disastrous upset.

Senior Zac Robinson was State's starting quarterback in 2009, which wasn't unexpected. After all, he had already set the school record for total offense his junior season.

In the 24-17 win over Texas Tech, though, Robinson took a hard hit that sidelined him. As the schedule would have it, the Pokes' next game was against 3-7 Colorado five days later, Thursday. The team's star quarterback would not make it back that quickly.

Head coach Mike Gundy went to the backup, who turned in "what had to be one of the worst halves by an OSU quarterback in recent memory." The first-half stat sheet showed no completions, one interception. In the press box at halftime, the consensus was clear: Gundy would have to put Robinson back in to save the 8-2 Cowboys' season.

Instead, the head coach unexpectedly resorted to Weeden, a sophomore who had been "banished to third-string status this entire season." Weeden was so surprised by the move that he had to run onto the field quickly so he could find his helmet. Not expecting to play, he had worn a baseball cap into the locker room.

Weeden had all of four minutes to warm up. He managed to get off five or six warm-up passes before he "was thrown right into the game." He was nervous all right. "You always got butterflies," he said. "I was excited. It was fun to get out there."

It was fun indeed. The quarterback who would lead OSU to two of its greatest seasons ever and set the school single-season record for passing yards unexpectedly led the Cowboys to a 31-28 win. He went 10-for-15 for 168 yards and two touchdowns.

Just like Colorado in 2009, we're pretty sure we've got everything figured out and under control, and then something unexpected like Brandon Weeden happens. About the only thing we can expect from life with any certainty is the unexpected.

God is that way too, suddenly showing up to remind us he's still around. A friend who calls and tells you he's praying for you, a hug from your child or grandchild, a lone lily that blooms in your yard -- unexpected moments when the divine comes crashing into our lives with such clarity that it takes our breath away and brings tears to our eyes.

But why shouldn't God do the unexpected? The only factor limiting what God can do in our lives is the paucity of our own faith. We should expect the unexpected from God, this same deity who caught everyone by surprise by unexpectedly coming to live among us as a man, and who will return when we least expect it.

*Surprised may be the right word. He just hadn't been out there enough.*
*-- Mike Gundy's reaction to Brandon Weeden's unexpected success*

**God continually does the unexpected,**
**like showing up as Jesus,**
**who will return unexpectedly.**

# THE PRIZE

**Read Philippians 3:10-16.**

*"I press on toward the goal to win the prize for which God has called me heavenward in Christ Jesus" (v. 14).*

**W**hen Barry Sanders was announced as the winner of the 1988 Heisman Trophy, he wasn't even in the country.

Sanders, Troy Aikman, Rodney Peete, Major Harris, and Steve Walsh were invited to the Heisman ceremony in New York City on Dec. 3. Sanders had an acceptable excuse for not being there; the Pokes were playing their season finale against Texas Tech in Tokyo, Japan. His parents and his brother went to New York on his behalf.

Not surprisingly, the CBS folks in Toyko wanted to broadcast Sanders' reaction to the announcement, especially if he won. That was a problem; because of the time difference, Sanders would have to make his appearance about 4 a.m. He was not too happy about the prospect of being roused out of bed that early with a game to be played some seven hours later.

Somebody came up with the idea of inviting the offensive linemen and fullback Garrett Limbrick to the TV studio to entice Sanders to come along. Head coach Pat Jones gave instructions to have the group ride in limos to prevent having to stuff all those big linemen into cabs. He also told the TV people to have plenty of coffee, doughnuts, and breakfast items on hand.

Jones insisted to the TV folks that the players all get in and out of the studio in a hurry because of the pre-game preparations. They said Sanders would simply say a few words if he won. Jones insisted there be no interviews; the TV folks agreed. Of course, Sanders won and he spoke his piece. Then to Jones' consternation, Bob Costas announced from New York that after a commercial they would have a live interview with Sanders. Jones literally pulled the plug on that idea. He yanked a handful of plugs out of a nearby wall, "and we got out of there."

Even the most modest and self-effacing among us like Barry Sanders can't help but be pleased by prizes and honors. They symbolize the approval and appreciation of others, whether it's an Employee of the Month trophy, a plaque for sales achievement, or the sign declaring yours as the neighborhood's prettiest yard.

Such prizes and awards are often the culmination of the pursuit of personal achievement and accomplishment. They represent accolades and recognition from the world. Nothing is inherently wrong with any of that as long as we keep them in perspective.

That is, we must never let awards become such idols that we worship or lower our sight from the greatest prize of all and the only one truly worth winning. It's one that won't rust, collect dust, or leave us wondering why we worked so hard to win it in the first place. The ultimate prize is eternal life, and it's ours through Jesus Christ.

*It was a big deal for us to be in Japan, and it was a big deal for them to have a Heisman Trophy winner present.*
*-- Pat Jones on being in Tokyo the day of the Heisman announcement*

**God has the greatest prize of all ready
to hand to you through Jesus Christ.**

# DRY RUN

**Read John 4:1-15.**

*"Everyone who drinks this water will be thirsty again,*
*but whoever drinks the water I give him will never thirst.*
*Indeed, the water I give him will become in him a spring*
*of water welling up to eternal life" (vv. 13-14).*

**Y**ou would think a wrestling program that at the time had won 27 national titles wouldn't experience a drought. In the case of Oklahoma State, you would be wrong.

As the Cowboys began the 1989 NCAA championships, they had not won a national title since 1971. With a lineup boasting six All-Americas, they were the top-seeded team. So had they been, though, in 1984 and '88 when they had finished second and fourth respectively.

This time was different; the team had a star to lead it in junior Kendall Cross. Described as "a campus heartthrob with soulful eyes," Cross was also "blessed with such stunning flexibility that his teammates call[ed] him Gumby."

Cross won the individual title at 126 pounds, but that was only after he appeared defeated in his quarterfinal match. He trailed 8-7 with time running out. "I thought I was beaten," he said. "I thought he would stay on my legs and ride it out." His opponent tried, but with four seconds left, the referee penalized him a point for stalling. Cross then won the match in the overtime.

In the semis, Cross met an Iowa wrestler who had beaten him

soundly earlier in the season. This time, Cross scored a point in the second period for an escape and held on for the 1-0 win. As the match ended, the frustrated wrestler shoved Cross in the back. He demonstrated his amazing flexibility when he tucked into a somersault and came up waving to the Iowa fans.

Joining Cross in winning an individual title was junior Chris Barnes, who would win a second title in 1990. By the time Cross wrestled for his title, the Pokes had already won the team championship. The drought was over.

You can walk across that river you boated on in the spring. The city's put all neighborhoods on water restriction. That beautiful lawn you fertilized and seeded will turn a sickly, pale green and may lapse all the way to brown. Somebody wrote "Wash Me" on the rear window of your truck.

The sun bakes everything, including the concrete. The earth itself seems exhausted, just barely hanging on. It's a drought.

It's the way a soul that shuts God out looks.

God instilled the physical sensation of thirst in us to warn us of our body's need for water. He also gave us a spiritual thirst that can be quenched only by his presence in our lives. Without God, we are like tumbleweeds, dried out and windblown, offering the illusion of life where there is only death.

Living water – water of life – is readily available in Jesus. We may drink our fill, and thus we slake our thirst and end our soul's drought – forever.

*Never's a long time. I guess 'never' is today.*
*-- OSU coach Joe Seay responding to a taunt that he'd never beat Iowa*

**Our soul thirsts for God's refreshing presence.**

# A ROARING SUCCESS

**Read Galatians 5:16-26.**

*"So I say, live by the Spirit. . . . The sinful nature desires what is contrary to the Spirit. . . . I warn you, as I did before, that those who live like this will not inherit the kingdom of God" (vv. 16, 17, 21).*

Sometimes a player's success and what he means to a program can't be measured by statistics alone. Such was the case of Xavier Lawson-Kennedy.

The defensive tackle wrapped up his Cowboy football career with the 2006 Independence Bowl. It was the 45th game of his college playing days. He went into that last game with a total of 36 tackles and one half of one sack -- for his four seasons. Such statistics are not usually indicators of football success.

Lawson-Kenndy's biggest impact on the Cowboy program un-doubtedly came before he arrived on campus. A five-star recruit rated as the No. 4 defensive tackle in the country, he announced his decision to play for State on Fox Sports' *Southwest Sports Report*. With that one moment, "We got national recognition," head coach Mike Gundy said. "It strengthened our position in recruiting."

In the summer before his freshman season, however, Lawson-Kennedy underwent knee surgery, and he never got over it. The injury limited the tackle's role on the field. "He couldn't control his weight," Gundy said. "It all just kind of snowballed."

"I will remember [him] as a team guy who did everything he

possibly could to get on the field," assistant head coach Joe De-Forest said. "He has been a leader. And he really was productive in what we asked him to do on the field."

So, although the stats don't show it, Lawson-Kennedy was a success on the field, doing everything he could to help the Cowboys win. He was successful in the classroom, too, maintaining a high grade-point average and graduating on time.

Are you a successful person? Your answer, of course, depends upon how you define success, as is the case with Xavier Lawson-Kennedy. Is the measure of your success based on the number of digits in your bank balance, the square footage of your house, that title on your office door, the size of your boat?

Certainly the world determines success by wealth, fame, prestige, awards, and possessions. Our culture screams that life is all about gratifying your own needs and wants. If it feels good, do it. It's basically the Beach Boys' philosophy of life.

But all success of this type has one glaring shortcoming: You can't take it with you. Eventually, Daddy takes the T-bird away. Like life itself, all these things are fleeting.

A more lasting way to approach success is through the spiritual rather than the physical. The goal becomes not money or backslaps by sycophants but eternal life spent with God. Success of that kind is forever.

*He never misses a class and he does everything right. In a business sense, he'll be very successful.*
*-- Mike Gundy on Xavier Lawson-Kennedy*

**Success isn't permanent, and failure isn't fatal --**
**unless it's in your relationship with God.**

# FOOD FOR THOUGHT

**Read Genesis 9:1-7.**

*"Everything that lives and moves will be food for you. Just as I gave you the green plants, I now give you everything"* *(v. 3).*

**W**aiting out a lengthy delay caused by bad weather, the Cowboy football team got hungry. Peanut butter and jelly sandwiches came to the rescue.

Toward the end of the pre-game warmups in Tulsa on Sept. 17, 2011, a huge line of thunderstorms moved over the stadium. Tulsa officials decided to delay the start; within a few minutes, sheets of rain, thunder, lightning, and hail bombarded the field.

The Cowboys were safely tucked away in the visitor's quarters, which was described as an "old cement bunker of a dressing room." The initial estimate was that the delay would last 30 minutes to an hour, but then the storm stalled right over the stadium.

The OSU coaches soon realized they had a problem. The kickoff had been moved to 9 p.m. for TV; the team's pre-game meal had been at 5:30. As the delay stretched into its second hour, the energy bars the strength staff had brought and the Cheetos some of the defensive backs had pulled out of their travel bags were long gone. The Cowboys were hungry.

Someone pointed out that a convenience store across the street probably had the ingredients necessary for an injection of peanut butter and jelly sandwiches. Fortunately, this was a road game for the coaches' wives. So when the strength staff returned with their booty, the wives turned a nearby media room into a makeshift kitchen. They even took requests, cutting off the crust for some players just as they did for their own children. They made Justin Blackmon a jelly sandwich since he was allergic to peanuts.

The sandwiches did their job and so did the Cowboys as they eventually romped to a 59-33 win to up their record to 3-0.

Belly up to the buffet, boys and girls, for barbecue, sirloin steak, grilled chicken, and a whole array of desserts from cake to cookies. Rachael Ray's a household name; hamburger joints, pizza parlors, and taco stands lurk on every corner; and we have a TV channel devoted exclusively to food. We love our chow.

Food is one of God's really good ideas, but consider the complex divine plan that begins with a kernel and winds up with corn-on-the-cob slathered with butter and littered with salt. The creator of all life devised a downright fascinating and effective system in which living things are sustained and nourished physically through the sacrifice of other living things in a way similar to what Christ underwent to save us spiritually.

Whether it's fast food or home-cooked, practically everything we eat is a gift from God secured through a divine plan in which some plants and/or animals have given up their lives. Pausing to give thanks before we dive in seems the least we can do.

*We had peanut butter and jelly all over us, up our arms, . . . because it was just assembly line and we were making them as fast as we could.*
*-- Jennifer Singleton, wife of running backs coach Jemal Singleton*

**God's system nourishes us through the sacrifice of other living things; that's worth a thank-you.**

# ZINGERS

**Read Luke 20:9-19.**

*"The teachers of the law and the chief priests looked for a way to arrest him . . . because they knew he had spoken . . . against them" (v. 19).*

**S**ome Sooner fan went to a great deal of trouble and expense to insult Oklahoma A&M's best player. Bad move.

Bob Fenimore is a Cowboy legend. Former State head coach Les Miles once said he fit right in with Thurman Thomas and Barry Sanders. He was the school's first All-America (1944 and '45) back when it was still Oklahoma A&M and was the first Cowboy to be inducted into the College Football Hall of Fame.

Fenimore played a game very different from the one we enjoy today, an age of "fold-up leather helmets, no face masks and minimal padding." He played in a single-wing offense, which gave him the responsibilities of a quarterback and the duties of a tailback. In a time when even the stars went both ways, he played safety and set the school record with 18 career interceptions. To top it off, Fenimore was the team's punter.

He led the Pokes to an undefeated season in 1945 that ended with a 33-13 win over the St. Mary's Gaels in the 1946 Sugar Bowl. The regular season ended with a 47-0 Bedlam victory in Norman, a game for which the Cowboys had a little extra motivation.

During the week of the game, a plane buzzed the A&M practice field and dumped several hundred leaflets on the players. "My number was 55," Fenimore recalled, "and they had this big old dumb-looking football player with 55 on his jersey, and down at the bottom they had 'OU 55, Oklahoma A&M 0.'" The insult only inspired the Cowboys to vow to win the game 55-0.

They nearly made it. When they led 47-0, head coach Jim Lookabaugh realized they couldn't make it to 55 in this day before the two-point conversion, so he called off the starters.

There's nothing like a ripping good insult to rile us up as it did the Cowboy football players in 1945. We take an insult exactly as it is meant: personally.

Few people throughout history can match Jesus, of all people, for delivering a well-placed zinger, and few insults throughout history can match the one he tossed at the religious authorities in Luke 20. Jesus' remarks were so accurate and so severe that the targets of his insult responded by seeking to have him arrested.

Using a vineyard as the centerpiece of an extensive allegory, Jesus insulted the priests and their lackeys by declaring that they had insulted God in rejecting his rule over them. They had sought to own God's kingdom for themselves.

They were truly just a bunch of hypocrites. But before we get too smug, we need to take a good look around. Little has changed. We still seek to live our lives on our terms, not God's. The world is in such a mess because we want to run God's vineyard, instead of surrendering to him. Jesus delivered that insult right at us.

*We decided we were going to go down and try to beat them 55-0.*
*-- Bob Fenimore on the team's response to his being insulted*

**In insulting the priests for rebelling against God,**
**Jesus delivered a zinger right at us.**

DAY 92

# THE END

**Read Revelation 22:7-21.**

*"I am the Alpha and the Omega, the First and the Last, the Beginning and the End" (v. 13).*

For nine seasons, Larry and Juana Woods had a son playing football for Oklahoma State. That remarkable run finally ended with the Insight Bowl of Dec. 31, 2007.

Two-time All-American wide receiver Rashaun Woods started the run with a redshirt season in 1999. Eventually an All-Big 12 receiver, D'Juan joined his older sibling in Stillwater in 2002, and after D'Juan received a medical redshirt, the brothers played together in 2003. The youngest Woods brother, Donovan, a quarterback, was also on the team that season. The trio never played together, however, because Donovan was redshirted.

Donovan quarterbacked the Cowboys to a 7-5 season and a berth in the Alamo Bowl in 2004. But after two games of the 2005 season, head coach Mike Gundy gave the starting slot to Bobby Reid and moved Donovan to the secondary. As a safety in 2006, Woods had 62 tackles. He moved again in 2007, starting as an outside linebacker.

With the Insight Bowl, Woods was in the State starting lineup for the 43rd and final time. The game also marked the end of a remarkable streak: It was the 108th straight and final time that the Woods parents attended an OSU game to watch a son play.

"I remember when we first started going to Stillwater on a

regular basis," Juana said. "This is a bittersweet time for our family." Mom and dad had talked about the bowl game being the end of an exciting and cherished time in their lives. They decided, as Juana said, "to go to the bowl game, . . . [to] take as many friends as possible, [and to] enjoy it and go out with a bang."

Donovan certainly did. In the bowl, the Cowboys thrashed the Hoosiers of Indiana 49-33. The youngest Woods sibling capped his family's nine-year run by logging nine tackles and being named the defensive MVP.

The string of games played by the three Woods brothers is just another example of one of life's basic truths: Everything ends. Even the stars have a life cycle, though admittedly it's rather lengthy. Erosion eventually will wear a boulder to a pebble. Life itself is temporary; all living things have a beginning and an end.

Within the framework of our individual lives, we experience endings. Loved ones, friends, and pets die; relationships fracture; jobs dry up; our health, clothes, lawn mowers, TV sets – they all wear out. Even this world as we know it will end.

But one of the greatest ironies of God's gift of life is that not even death is immune from the great truth of creation that all things must end. That's because through Jesus' life, death, and resurrection, God himself acted to end any power death once had over life. In other words, because of Jesus, the end of life has ended. Eternity is ours for the claiming.

*It is a good way to end it.*
*-- Defensive MVP Donovan Woods after the Insight Bowl*

**Everything ends; thanks to Jesus Christ, so does death.**

**THE END    185**

# A Note or Two from the Author to the Fans of the Cowboys

Okay, Oklahoma State fans, I'll let you in on a little secret. I'm a die-hard Georgia Bulldogs fan, and I'm not sure I've ever gotten over that rude spanking your Cowboys handed my Dawgs in the 2009 season opener. As much as it pained me, I managed to write Devotion No. 45 about that game without shedding too many tears.

I'll let you in on something else, too, that shouldn't be a secret to you. I'm a Christian. Jesus Christ is the Lord and Savior of my life. That means I live each day in joy even when the world hands me setbacks, such as the Bulldogs getting soundly whipped.

Despite my rapidly advancing years, I still remain dismayed by people who reject Jesus. I don't know how they make it. I have no idea why God has heaped such inordinate blessings upon me in my life as he has. My wife and I are healthy, I have a son and two healthy grandsons, my two sisters are still kicking, and I was close to my mother and my father until the moment of their deaths, each having lived productive lives.

As we all do, though, I have friends and acquaintances whose lives have not been free of tragedy, heartbreak, and debilitating disease. How does anyone make it through life without surrendering to despair, addiction, and/or bitterness and hatred if they don't have Jesus to lean upon?

It's not so clear-cut, of course, but in a way these devotion books are my pitiable little offer of thanksgiving to God. They also are, I am convinced, God's way of thanking me. Let another secret be revealed, one that I never kept from the congregations I pastored: I never, ever wanted to enter the ministry. Who was I to be a so-called Man of God? It would only be a matter of time before I was revealed as a fraud. You see, I haven't always been a nice boy.

Hey, I was a journalist and a college professor most of my sentient life. I'm not slandering my former colleagues, I don't think, when

I suggest that the two professions aren't exactly fecund breeding grounds for men of the cloth. Preaching? Counseling? Teaching the Bible? Not me, bub.

So I pulled a Jonah. I ran from God's call upon my life. Though I never had an encounter with a big fish, I finally realized, like Jonah, that God wasn't going anywhere. I gave up; I surrendered. And this unworthy vessel, this wretched sinner, this reluctant pastor entered upon his life's most glorious phase. My only regret was all those years -- not lost, but not spent in the awesome glory of serving God.

All my adult life, the only goal I sought after was to write a book and have it published. That's why I say these books are God's gift to me even as I offer them up to God and to you. When I quit seeking what I wanted and instead devoted my life to what he wanted for me, God handed me everything of which I had dreamed.

I suggest you try it, this difficult surrendering stuff. Each one of us has a ministry God has placed upon us. It may not be full-time ministry, especially pulpit ministry. Only you can know the way in which God is speaking to your heart. I can only give you my example to help you decide.

If you're reading this page, then you've read the book. My fondest prayer for these devotions is that they offer you some enjoyment, recall a few precious memories, draw a smile or two, and provide a little insight into and depth for your faith.

Keep on pullin' for the Pokes -- and look me up in Heaven when we're all sitting at the feet of Jesus. We can rehash that '09 game.

Have faith! Have fun! Go Cowboys! Go God!

Ed McMinn

# NOTES
## (by Devotion Day Number)

1   In the spring of 1934, a . . . and he took it.: John Paul Bischoff, *Mr. Iba: Basketball's Aggie Iron Duke* (Oklahoma City: Oklahoma Heritage Association, 1980), p. 83.

1   The Oklahoma press proclaimed . . . could work miracles overnight.": Bischoff, *Mr. Iba*, p. 86.

1   The student newspaper scathingly . . . Missouri Valley Conference.": Bischoff, *Mr. Iba*, p. 86.

1   The gym was not adequate . . . the program consistently lost money.: Bischoff, *Mr. Iba*, p. 85.

1   They weren't tall, and . . . a winning season in 1935.: Bischoff, *Mr. Iba*, p. 87.

1   His 'glum forecasts' prophesied no better than a .500 season ahead.: Bischoff, *Mr. Iba*, p. 87.

2   In high school during a . . . there were four of them.": Jenni Carlson, "Former OSU Football Coach Jim Stanley Dies," *NewsOK.com*, Jan. 12, 2012, newsok.com/former-osu-football-coach-jim-stanley-dies/article/3639689.

2   part of Stanley's pre-game . . . he wouldn't tell you.": Carlson, "Former OSU Football Coach Jim Stanley Dies."

2   He was an extremely tough individual and very hard-nosed.: Carlson, "Former OSU Football Coach Jim Stanley Dies."

3   Cowgirl third baseman Mariah . . . or people getting on you.": Christopher Shelton, "OSU Athletes Reveal Unique Habits," *Stillwater NewsPress*, June 6, 2009, http://www.stwnewspress.com/osusports/x1627934.

3   I could tell you bazillion, but some are dumber than others.: Shelton, "OSU Athletes Reveal Unique Habits."

4   Even the coach admitted the whole situation was "a little odd.": George Schroeder, "At Oklahoma State, The Student Became the Teacher this Spring," *SI.com*, April 15, 2011. http://sportsillustrated.cnn.com/2011/writers/george_schroeder/04/14.

4   The team needed "to . . . without the architect.": Schroeder, "At Oklahoma State."

4   having a new offensive . . . "was a little tricky.": Schroeder, "At Oklahoma State."

4   Monken "was willing to . . . making 60 people adjust.": Schroeder, "At Oklahoma State."

4   "He's gotta be involved . . . anybody in the building.": Schroeder, "At Oklahoma State."

4   We're kind of piecing it together.: Schroeder, "At Oklahoma State."

5   "I had seen all the turnovers I wanted to see,": Pat Jones with Jimmie Tramel, *Pat Jones' Tales from Oklahoma State Football* (Champaign, Ill.: Sports Publishing L.L.C., 2007), p. 123.

5   "We loved [Williams], but . . . to get Mike going,": Jones with Tramel, *Pat Jones' Tales*, p. 125.

5   at halftime, Jones told Gundy he was in.: Jones with Tramel, *Pat Jones' Tales*, p. 123.

5   He first sailed his helmet across the locker room: Jones with Tramel, *Pat Jones' Tales*, p. 124.

5   "Ronnie handled it about . . . time I was there,": Jones with Tramel, *Pat Jones' Tales*, p. 125.

5   Of all the guys . . . for than Ronnie Williams.: Jones with Tramel, *Pat Jones' Tales*, p. 125.

6   "We came out in the second . . . postgame celebration at midfield.: Rhett Morgan, "It's an Orange-Letter Day," *Tulsa World*, Nov. 9, 1997, http://tulsaworld.com/article.aspx/Its_an_Orange_Letter_Day_Cowboys_Swamp_Sooners_With_Historic_Victory/638532.

6   got his most extensive playing . . . since he couldn't stop smiling.: John E. Hoover, "Howell Shines in Rare Chance," *Tulsa World*, Nov. 9, 1997, http://tulsaworld.com/article.aspx/Howell_Shines_in_Rare_Chance/19971108.

7   with a salary of $4,500.: John Klein, "James Wadley Looking Forward to the View from the Stands," *Tulsa World*, May 3, 2012, www.tulsaworld.com/article/aspx/John-Klein-James-Wadley-looking-forward-to-the-view-from-the-stands/2012503_203_b1_james241659.

7   the move resulted in . . . apartment complex's laundry.: Berry Tramel, "Tennis Coach James Wadley Is OSU's Grand Old Man," *NewsOK.com*, Sept. 29, 2009, newsok.com/tennis-coach-james-wadley-is-osus-grand-old-man/article/3404086.

7   more than 60 head . . . over the tennis program.: Klein, "James Wadley Looking Forward."

7   In 2009, he told . . . is probably time for me.": John Klein, "James Wadley Looking Forward."

7   "That's what happens when . . . perfect for me.": Klein, "James Wadley Looking Forward."

7   "My wife thinks I'm . . . off in the summer.": Tramel, "Tennis Coach James Wadley."

7   He's older than Methuselah.: Tramel, "Tennis Coach James Wadley."

8    Quarterback Clint Chelf declared that . . . because he missed lunch.": Jason Elmquist, "Oklahoma State Football Finds Ways to Have Fun," *Stillwater NewsPress*, Dec. 28, 2012, www./stwnewspress.com/osusports/x503807920.

9    "one of [Oklahoma State's] most cherished football seasons.": Jimmie Tramel, "'One-Heart Team,'" *Tulsa World*, Sept. 11, 2001, http://www.tulsaworld.com/article.aspx/One_heart_team/010911_Sp_b1onehe.

9    "I thought we were one . . . the end of the year,": Jimmie Tramel, "'One-Heart Team.'"

9    That [Colorado loss] helped. . . of a one-heart team.: Jimmie Tramel, "'One-Heart Team.'"

10   "I'm going to remember this when I'm 70,": Dave Sittler, "OSU Will Remember Nov. 24, 2001, *Tulsa World*, Nov. 25, 2001, http://www.tulsaworld.com/article.aspx/OSU_will_remember_Nov_24_2001/L112501067.

10   a "stunning, monumental victory,": Sittler, "OSU Will Remember."

10   the biggest win in school history.: Sittler, "OSU Will Remember."

10   "showing uncommon cool in a red-hot moment.": Dan O'Kane, "OU KO'd," *Tulsa World*, Nov. 25, 2001, http://www.tulsaworld.com/article.aspx/OU_KOd/L112501098.

10   "I thought all along we . . . a chance to win.": John Klein, "Bedlam Became a Shocker," *Tulsa World*, Nov. 25, 2001, http://www.tulsaworld.com/article.aspx/L112501097.

10   This is something OSU . . . will remember forever.: Klein, "Bedlam Becomes a Shocker."

11   "an affable man with . . . and a startled laugh.": John Garrity, "They're Runnin' and Gunnin'," *Sports Illustrated*, Feb. 16, 1981, http://sportsillustrated.cnn.com/vault/article/magazine/MAG1124223/index.htm.

11   His family had barely . . . presumably stolen.: Garrity, "They're Runnin' and Gunnin'."

11   Hansen started feeling bad . . . goal of the game.: Garrity, "They're Runnin' and Gunnin'."

11   Hey, I'm a happy . . . are just going to happen.: Garrity, "They're Runnin' and Gunnin'."

12   DeForest had been somewhat . . . visions of going all the way.: Matt Doyle, "Cowboys Add a Trick to the Kick," *Tulsa World*, Oct. 12, 2003, http://www.tulsaworld.com/article.aspx/Cowboys_add_a_trick_to_the_kick/031012_Sp_b6_cow.

12   After the fake, the success of our offense was very evident.: John E. Hoover, "Right Back on Track," *Tulsa World*, Oct. 12, 2003, http://www.tulsaworld.com/article.aspx/Right_back_on_track/031012_Sp_b1_right.

13   "He just went up . . . enough, you can play,": Jones with Tramel, *Pat Jones' Tales*, p. 121.

13   [1986] was a hard-luck . . . we played at Houston.: Jones with Tramel, *Pat Jones' Tales*, p. 122.

14   At an Oklahoma State recruiting . . . his troublesome answer? "Nobody.": Jimmie Tramel, "Unheralded Recruit Now an Expected Oklahoma State Starter," *Tulsa World*, Aug. 20, 2013, http://www.tulsaworld.com/article.aspx/Unheralded_recruit_now_an_expected_Oklahoma_State_starter/20130820_93_B1_CUTLIN58363.

14   Wickline joked that. . . faith in our coaches,": Jimmie Tramel, "Unheralded Recruit."

14   "despicable, vile, unprincipled scoundrels.": John MacArthur, *Twelve Ordinary Men* (Nashville: W Publishing Group, 2002), p. 152.

14   He had the worst feet. . . . heavy or real strong.: Jimmie Tramel, "Unheralded Recruit."

15   Senior Alan Britton -- the NCAA . . . sudden death playoff.: Rick Lipsey, "Down to the Wire," *Sports Illustrated*, June 12, 1995, http://sportsillustrated.cnn.com/vault/article/magazine/MAG1006704/index.htm.

15   Sophomore Leif Westerberg had . . . and we're great friends.": Lipsey, "Down to the Wire."

15   What [Coach Mike Holder] makes us . . . to conquer the odds.: Lipsey, Down to the Wire."

16   touchdown that was called Oklahoma State's season-defining moment.": Chris Day, "Oklahoma State Fullback Kye Staley Finally Gets His Touchdown," *Stillwater NewsPress*, Oct. 30, 2011, http://www.stwnewspress.com/osusports/x783647696.

16   it left quarterback . . . heart, and teamwork.": Day, "Oklahoma State Fullback Kye Staley."

16   During 2009's fall camp, . . . to the game.: Day, "Oklahoma State Fullback Kye Staley."

16   During the week, offensive . . . I am right now.": Day, "Oklahoma State Fullback Kye Staley."

17   On the sideline as he waited . . . You've got no composure!": Bill Haisten, "Bobby Reid's Evolution," *Tulsa World*, Oct. 17, 2006, http://www.tulsaworld.com/article.aspx/Bobby_Reids_evolution/061017_Sp_B1_QBflo3835.

17   Reid took a moment . . . nothing to say.: Haisten, "Bobby Reid's Evolution."

17   I saw him sitting down. He wouldn't look at me.: Haisten, "Bobby Reid's Evolution."

18    "Those guys were so . . . and done really well.": Jones with Tramel, *Pat Jones' Tales*, p. 132.
18    "The score didn't do . . . the matchup was.": Jones with Tramel, *Pat Jones' Tales*, p. 140.
18    Late in the game, the . . . in the first place.": Jones with Tramel, *Pat Jones' Tales*, p. 140.
19    Oliver seemed to have won . . . that beat the buzzer.: Gary R. Blockus, "Jordan Oliver Seeks Second NCAA Wrestling Championship," *The Morning Call*, March 19, 2013, http://articles.mcall.com/2013-03-19/sports/mc-oliver-wrestling-nationals-03192013-2013.
19    "an egregious no-call by the referee.": Jason Elmquist, "Oliver's Win Cements Wrestling Legacy at OSU," *Stillwater NewsPress*, March 26, 2013, http://www.stwnewspress.com. osusports/x149931924.
19    "It's definitely not the outcome . . . decisive on the scoreboard.": Blockus, "Jordan Oliver."
19    I have bitter feeling about that.: Blockus, "Jordan Oliver."
20    "outplayed OU from start . . . coaching -- every phase.": John E. Hoover, "97th Bedlam Battle: It's No Fluke," *Tulsa World*, Dec. 1, 2002, http://www.tulsaworld.com/article. aspx/97th_Bedlam_Battle_Its_no_Fluke/021201_Sp_B1_itsno.
20    "Two years in a row . . . that's unbelievable,": Hoover, "97th Bedlam Battle."
20    "What a great feeling,": Hoover, "97th Bedlam Battle."
20    You should always fear the underdogs.: John Klein, "OSU Salts Wound," *Tulsa World*, Dec. 1, 2002, http://www.tulsaworld.com/article.aspx/OSU_salts_wound/021201_Ne_a1_ twice.
21    The husband, Rusty, attended . . . were actually really mad.": Bill Haisten, "A House United," *Tulsa World*, Nov. 22, 2007, http://www.tulsaworld.com/article.aspx/A_ house_united/071122_238_B1_hThef11578.
21    Mom and dad finally . . . Fedora won him over.: Haisten, "A House United."
21    "I bleed orange.": Haisten, "A House United."
21    It was definitely a house divided. But not anymore.: Haisten, "A House United."
22    There was every reason to . . . of the Les Miles era.": John Klein, "Cowboys Change Direction." *Tulsa World*, Oct. 24, 2004, www.tulsaworld.com/article.aspx/Cowboys_change_ direction/041024_Sp_B6_Cowboy36122.
22    "Personally, I thought we stunk,": Mike Brown, "Running Directly at Their Challenge," *Tulsa World*, Oct. 24, 2004, http://www.tulsaworld.com/article.aspx.Running_directly_ at_their_challenge/041024/Sp_b7_Runni3657.
22    He followed Sam Mayes . . . out the defensive end.: Brown, "Running Directly."
22    I've got faith in my . . . were going to get it done.: Bill Haisten, "OSU Kicks Back," *Tulsa World*, Oct. 24, 2004. http://tulsaworld.com/article.aspx/OSU_kicks_back/04024_Sp_ B7_OSUki55637.
23    "an unlikely bunch of players,": William F. Reed, "Rough and Ready," *Sports Illustrated*, March 11, 1991, http://sportsillustrated.cnn.com/vault/article/magazine/MAG1118947/ index.htm.
23    It got so bad that the . . . "into a frenzied zoo": Reed, "Rough and Ready."
23    "told us that if we . . . next day and run five miles.": Reed, "Rough and Ready."
23    I guess we can put our running shoes back on the rack.: Reed, "Rough and Ready."
24    "We made mistakes, we . . . could a little gun shy,": Robert Allen and Mike Gundy, *More Than a Championship* (Oklahoma City: Oklahoma Heritage Association: 2012), p. 169.
24    the locker room at halftime . . . "You just sensed they were fine,": Allen and Gundy, p. 160.
24    When you have a football . . . then you can [come from behind].: Allen and Gundy, p. 169.
25    "the greatest one-man offense in college football history.": "Bob Fenimore, All-American at OSU, Dies at Age 84," *Tulsa World*, July 28, 2010, http://www.tulsaworld.com/article. aspx/Bob_Fenimore_All_American_at_OSU_dies_at_age_84/20100728_93_0_bob fen873290.
25    Armstrong also had the picture . . . the officials, they shook hands.: "Cowboy Football: Remembering a Cowboy Legend," okstate.com, Sept. 8, 2010, http://www.okstate.com/ sports/m-footbal/spec-rel/090810aab.html.
25    That was just a special . . . with a teammate.: "Cowboy Football: Remembering."
26    For the first time in . . . more than 100 yards rushing.: Bill Haisten, "OSU Tops Tech," *Tulsa World*, Sept. 23, 2007, http://www.tulsaworld.com/article.aspx/OSU_tops_ Tech/070923_Z_B11_ENWor78485.
26    The Raider quarterback thought his pass was good for six;: Matt Doyle, "Final Defensive

Play Saves Cowboys," *Tulsa World*, Sept. 23, 2007, http://www.tulsaworld.com/article. aspx/Final_defensive_play_saves_Cowboys/070923_Z_B19_hrbri10720.

26    I don't think you . . . fortunate not to lose.: Jerry Kirshenbaum, ed., "They Said It," *Sports Illustrated*, Oct. 8, 1984, http://sportsillustrated.cnn.com/vault/article/magazine/ MAG1122687/index.htm.

27    Defensive coordinator Pat Jones declared. . . in Stillwater in 1983.: Jones with Tramel, p. 48.

27    "a legit middle linebacker in our 4-3 defense.": Jones with Tramel, *Pat Jones' Tales*, p. 48.

27    The scrambling OSU . . . to inside linebacker.: Jones with Tramel, *Pat Jones' Tales*, p. 48.

27    an add-on in the . . . completed the front line.: Jones with Tramel, *Pat Jones' Tales*, p. 49.

27    If Krebs doesn't break . . . Probably not.: Jones with Tramel, *Pat Jones' Tales*, p. 50.

28    Sophomore Megan Byford realized . . . "It was just . . . amazing,": Gina Mizell, "Oklahoma State Women's Basketball," *NewsOK.com*, Feb. 22, 2013, http://newsok.com/oklahoma-state-womens-basketball-2008-bedlam-win-turned-the-tide-for-cowgirls-basketball/ article/3758229.

28    "changed the program." . . . of the Big 12 anymore.": Mizell, "Oklahoma State."

28    It's one of the greatest moments of my life.: Mizell, "Oklahoma State."

29    it was a Stillwater convenience . . . to still have my life.: Jimmie Tramel, "OSU's Golden Thankful," *The Tulsa World*, Aug. 31, 1999, http://www.tulsaworld.com/article.aspx/ OSUs_Golden_thankful/ 1990830_Sp_b7osuse.

29    Golden found that sitting . . . have been here.": Jimmie Tramel, "OSU's Golden Thankful."

29    He's ready to go. . . . eager all summer.: Jimmie Tramel, "OSU's Golden Thankful."

30    "We had a good team. . . . "They had great players.": John Klein, "20 Years Ago, Aggie Defense Was Destroyed," *Tulsa World*, Oct. 3, 2008, http://www.tulsaworld.com/ article.aspx/20_years_ago_Aggie_defense_was_destroyed/20081003_203_B1_ BARRYS473786.

30    On third and long, . . . "We didn't even touch him.": Klein, "20 Years Ago."

30    "To see the way he ran through us was pretty amazing,": Klein, "20 Years Ago."

30    I really didn't know much . . . by the end of that game.: Klein, "20 Years Ago."

31    Bell and the OSU offense ran . . . to get my 1,000,'": John E. Hoover, "Bell's Long Smile Tops 1,000 Yards," *Tulsa World*, Dec. 28, 2002, http://www.tulsaworld.com/article.aspx/ Bells_long_smile_tops_1000_yards/021228_Sp_89_bells.

31    Bell followed a block from senior fullback Mike Denard: Hoover, "Bell's Long Smile."

31    I wanted to be the leading . . . be a 1,000-yard back.: Hoover, "Bell's Long Smile."

32    "re-established the dominance of OSU over the rest of the wrestling world.": "Oklahoma State Cowboys Wrestling," *Wikipedia, the free encylopedia*, http://en.wikipedia.org/ wiki/Oklahoma_State_Cowboys_wrestling.

32    No other school has . . . established to wrestling.: "Cowboy Wrestling: Dynasty Defined," *okstate.com*, http://www.okstate.com/sports/m-wrestl/spec-rel/wr-tradition.html.

33    Colton Chelf made a fingertip . . . for the end zone.: Allen with Gundy, p. 293.

33    On the sideline, defensive end . . . going to make this kick,": Allen with Gundy, p. 294.

33    I was thinking, 'Quinn . . . get my hat and shirt.': Allen with Gundy, p. 294.

34    During his collegiate days, he . . . fish out of the toilet,": Jimmie Tramel, "Country Boy at Heart," *Tulsa World*, Nov. 6, 2001, http://www.tulsaworld.com/article.aspx/Country_ boy_at_heart/1011105_Sp_b1woods.

34    He would rather fish than eat.: Jimmie Tramel, "Country Boy at Heart."

35    Not too much was expected . . . had never lifted weights;: Craig Neff, "The Importance of Ernest," *Sports Illustrated*, Oct. 25, 1982, http://sportsillustrated.cnn.com/vault/article/ magazine/MAG1126040/index.htm.

35    "That freshman year was . . . beside his father.: Neff, "The Importance of Ernest."

35    We knew last year . . . needed him there to block.: Neff, "The Importance of Ernest."

36    he went on Cowboy road . . . "blowtorches and all,": Grant Wahl, "Portrait of the Artist," *Sports Illustrated*, March 13, 2000, http://sportsillustrated.cnn.com/vault/article/ magazine/MAG1018524/index.htm.

36    On a blazing Texas summer . . .with no ill effects at all.: Wahl, "Portrait of the Artist."

36    Desmond [Mason] does things . . . aren't supposed to do.: Wahl, "Portrait of the Artist."

37    "alternating brilliance with misery": John Klein, "Cowboys Cap Season

with Thriller," *Tulsa World*, Dec. 29, 2006, http://www.tulsaworld.com/article.aspx/ Cowboys_cap_season_with_thriller/061229_Sp_B1_Cowbo9042.

37    "I just thought we were . . . we had been all year,": Klein, "Cowboys Cap Season."

37    "Nobody was panicking,": Bill Haisten, "Fine Finale," *Tulsa World*, Dec. 29, 2006, http:// www.tulsaworld.com/article.aspx/Fine_finale/061229_Sp_B1_Lated28541.

37    "I told the guys it . . . what we had to do.": Klein, "Cowboys Cap Season."

37    "It is evident [we] learned . . . how to overcome adversity.: Klein, "Cowboys Cap Season."

38    "The Sun Bowl people . . . do the same thing,": Jones with Tramel, *Pat Jones' Tales*, p. 143.

38    but two months later . . . up to his tall tale.: Jones with Tramel, *Pat Jones' Tales*, p. 144.

38    I went through the . . . a bill for those boots.: Jones with Tramel, *Pat Jones' Tales*, p. 144.

39    Blackmon was 8 years old . . . with the marching band.: Dan Greene, "Southwest Success Story," *Sports Illustrated*, 12 Aug. 2011, http://sportsillustrated.cnn.com/vault/articles/ magazine/MAG1188655/index.htm.

39    On April 23, 2011, that . . . lined up for his autograph.: Greene, "Southwest Success Story."

39    Someone proposed that a street be named for him.: Olin Buchanan, "Blackmon Making a Name for Himself," *rivals.com*, May 5, 2011, http://collegefootball.rivals.com/content. asp?CID=1218606.

39    "It was a homecoming . . . couldn't find on a map.": Greene, 'Southwest Success Story."

39    Things would be a lot . . . I'm glad we did.: Greene, "Southwest Success Story."

40    Guerrero's dad wrestled in . . . Guerreo got beat,: Austin Murphy, "Slick and Oh-So Quick," *Sports Illustrated*, March 22, 1999, http:''sportsillustrated.cnn.com/vault/article/ magazine/MAG1015361/index.htm.

40    Smith was impressed . . . tomorrow's another day.'": Murphy, "Slick and Oh-So Quick."

41    His ankle rolled over as . . . he couldn't feel his legs.: Terry Tush, "Artrell Woods Talks About Injury," *GoPokes*, Aug. 4, 2007, http://oklahomastate.scout.com/2/664695.html.

41    doctors remained unsure whether . . . I gave God the glory.": Bill Haisten, "Comeback Cowboy," *Tulsa World*, Aug. 29, 2008, http://www.tulsaworld.com/article.aspx/ Comeback_Cowboy/20080829_93_B1_OSUwid878851.

41    "nothing short of a miracle.": Tush, "Artrell Woods Talks About Injury."

41    "I've had some days . . . teammates visited him.: Tush, "Artrell Woods Talks About Injury."

41    "It's a pretty amazing story,": Haisten, "Comeback Cowboy."

41    The crowd gave him a standing . . . joining in the applause.: Scott Munn, "State College Notebook: Former OSU Wide Receiver Artrell Woods at UCO," *NewsOK.com*, Aug. 4, 2010, http://newsok.com/state-college-notebook-former-osu-wide-receiver-artrell-woods-at-uco/article/3482389.

41    I knew [God] was going . . . point, sooner or later.: Haisten, "Comeback Cowboy."

42    With the ball at the . . . before he was tackled.: Rhett Morgan, "Cowboys Get Mile-High Lift," *Tulsa World*, Oct. 12, 1997, http://www.tulsaworld.com/articles.aspx/Cowboys_ Get_Mile_High_Lift_Lindsay_Mayes_TD_Pass_Reels/634784.

43    *ESPN on ABC* rolled into . . . and Kirk Herbstreit in tow.: Allen and Gundy, p. 175.

43    In the locker room before . . . high the stakes were: Allen and Gundy, p. 177.

43    who led the team in prayer when they arrived at the stadium,: Allen and Gundy, p. 186.

43    When [OSU] fans in the . . . often as being instrumental.: Allen and Gundy, p. 182.

44    pretty much the same guys who had won the last two titles.: Barry McDermott, "A Wake for Wake Forest," *Sports Illustrated*, June 21, 1976, http://sportsillustrated.cnn.com/vault/ article/magazine/MAG1091235/index.htm.

44    Holder felt he had a lineup that could hang with Wake Forest.: McDermott, "A Wake for Wake Forest."

44    "a Brazilian with a . . . the country the year before.": McDermott, "A Wake for Wake Forest."

44    They were somewhat acclaimed . . . the greens into linoleum.": McDermott, "A Wake for Wake Forest."

44    When the top four . . . combined one over par,: McDermott, "A Wake for Wake Forest."

44    All this talk just . . . pressure on Wake Forest.: McDermott, "A Wake for Wake Forest."

45    No pressure,": Albert Chen, "Uprising in Stillwater," *Sports Illustrated*, Sept. 14, 2009, http:// sportsillustrated.cnn.com/vault/article/magazine/MAG1160023/index.htm.

45    The game of Sept. 5, . . . opener in school history.": Chen, "Uprising in Stillwater."

45    the program's highest preseason spot ever.: Chen, "Uprising in Stillwater."

45    In the spring, the Georgia . . . led to Gundy's quip,: Chen, "Uprising in Stillwater."

45    "In years past we would . . . no one flinched,": Chen, "Uprising in Stillwater."

46    "We knew we were going . . . we didn't know.": Jones with Tramel, *Pat Jones' Tales*, p. 74.

46    "They couldn't move the . . . ran wild on them,": Jones with Tramel, *Pat Jones' Tales*, p. 76.

46    He asked Jones if this . . . first game of his career.: Jones with Tramel, *Pat Jones' Tales*, p. 76.

46    [The reporter] acted like . . . but he didn't know it.: Jones wit h Tramel, *Pat Jones' Tales*, p. 76.

47    At that point, head coach . . . kids play. Garbage time.": John E. Hoover, "Miles' Decision
      Avoids Close Call," *Tulsa World*, Sept. 8, 2003, http://www.tulsaworld.com/article.
      aspx/Miles_decision_avoids_close_call/030908_Sp_b8_miles.

47    "If the second team . . . to go into the game.: Hoover, "Miles' Decision Avoids Close Call."

47    My mind was out . . . told me to go back in.: Hoover, "Miles' Decision Avoids Close Call."

48    In 1943, when Henry Iba . . . that he was crazy.: Bischoff, *Mr. Iba*, p. 141.

48    The prevailing philosophy among . . . as big as Robert Kurland, : Bischoff, *Mr. Iba*, p. 140.

48    Even Iba had his . . . the gangling player's attitude,: Bischoff, *Mr. Iba*, p. 139.

48    One coach called him "a . . . called Kurland a "glandular goon.": Bischoff, *Mr. Iba*, p. 141.

48    Because the military didn't . . . to be a goaltender,: Bischoff, *Mr. Iba*, p. 142.

48    When Iba headed East in . . . revolution in the game of basketball.": Bischoff, *Mr. Iba*, p. 144.

48    The sport was about to be surrendered to giants.: Bischoff, *Mr. Iba*, p. 144.

49    During the season, though, problems . . . a promise to uphold her.: S.L. Price, "The Gift,"
      *Sports Illustrated*. 6 July 1998. http://sportsillustrated.cnn.com/vault/article/magazine/
      MAG1013290/index.htm.

49    Before the procedure, Linda . . . miracle was at hand,": Price, "The Gift."

49    The surgeries went off . . . without breaking into tears.: Price, "The Gift."

49    I was trying to get him to understand this was a gift.: Price, "The Gift."

50    when the California boys . . . heavier than the Gaels." Marty Mule, "How Oklahoma
      A&M and St. Mary's Met in the 1946 Sugar Bowl," from *Sugar Bowl Classic: A History*,
      reprinted at http://allstatesugarbowl.org/site155.php.

50    With many of its . . . to Allied lines.: Mule, "How Oklahoma A&M and St. Mary's Met."

50    a Reynolds pass was . . . the deflection and scored.: Mule, "How Oklahoma A&M and St.
      Mary's Met."

50    We looked like midgets on the field.: Mule, "How Oklahoma A&M and St. Mary's Met."

51    He always insisted baseball . . . head football coach Les Miles,: Mark Beech, "State Secret,"
      *Sports Illustrated*, Oct. 18, 2004. http://sportsillustrated.cnn.com/vault/article/
      magazine/MAG1113275/index.htm.

51    "We rolled the dice and . . . them on and break them in,": Beech, "State Secret."

51    I don't understand it, but I'm all for it if it works.: Beech, "State Secret."

52    "a ragtag roster of transfers, junior college wanderers and injury-stricken sob stories,": John
      E. Hoover, "Back in the Saddle," *Tulsa World*, March 1, 2004, http://www.tulsaworld.
      com/article.aspx/Back_in_the_saddle/040302/Sp_b1_back.

52    "I'm kind of speechless . . . thought this would happen.": John E. Hoover, "Coronation
      Day," *Tulsa World*, March 7, 2004, http://www.tulsaworld.com/article.aspx/Corona-
      tion_day/040307_Sp_b1_coron.

52    These guys have certainly . . . to grow as a team.: Haisten, "Back in the Saddle."

53    "a perfect start for the Cowboys.": Bill Haisten, "How They Scored," *Tulsa World*, Oct. 14,
      2007, http://www.tulsaworld.com/article.aspx/How_They_Scored/071014_2_B16_
      hrbri640.

53    "the stat sheet was replete with remarkable numbers.": Bill Haisten, "Updated: Oklahoma
      State Blows Out Nebraska 45-14," *Tulsa World*, Oct. 13, 2007, http://www.tulsaworld.
      com/article.aspx/Updated_Oklahoma_State_blows_out_Nebraska_45_14/071013_
      2_LINCO85470.

54    Johnson was the last . . . enough for another day.: Jones with Tramel, *Pat Jones' Tales*, p. 3.

54    When Johnson landed the . . . spot, Jones said yes.: Jones with Tramel, *Pat Jones' Tales*, p. 2.

54    When the announcement . . . the Tangerine Bowl: Jones with Tramel, *Pat Jones' Tales*, p. 3.

54    During the week before . . . a little bit tense,": Jones with Tramel, *Pat Jones' Tales*, p. 3.

54    when Johnson and Jones . . . swipe any gear.: Jones with Tramel, *Pat Jones' Tales*,
      pp. 3-4.

54    That taught us that, . . . get on down the road.: Jones with Tramel, *Pat Jones'*

*Tales*, p. 3.

55    He was feeling "weird," . . . and "just kind of goofy.": John E. Hoover, "Having a Fields Day," *Tulsa World*, Nov. 17, 2002, http://www.tulsaworld.com/article.aspx/Having_a_ Fields_day/021117_Sp_B1_Havin.

55    "I thought it was going . . . thank you, Lord,": Hoover, "Having a Fields Day."

55    It's a great day for [Josh] Fields.": Hoover, "Having a Fields Day."

56    As an engineer, Gallagher . . . can do you no good.": Mark Palmer, "Ed Gallagher: Father of Intercollegiate Wrestling," *revwrestling.com*, July 31, 2008, reprinted at *okstate.com*, http://www.okstate.com/sports/m-wrestl/spec-rel/wr-tradition.html.

56    "We do not choose whether . . . on which we will stand.": R. Alan Culpepper, "The Gospel of Luke: Introduction, Commentary, and Reflections," *The New Interpreter's Bible*, Vol. IX (Nashville: Abingdon Press, 1998), p. 153.

56    [OSU] has built a wrestling . . . foundation is Ed Gallagher.: Mark Palmer, "Ed Gallagher."

57    the "most important home . . . Bedlam win over Oklahoma.": Bill Haisten, "OSU 41, Nebraska 29," *Tulsa World*, Oct. 29, 2006. http://www.tulsaworld.com/article.aspx/ OSU_41_Nebraska_29_OSU_pops_Corn/061029_Sp_B11_OSUov28266.

57    "It's a good day for Oklahoma State,": Haisten, "OSU 41, Nebraska 29."

57    "but the Cowboy offense . . . Nebraska was doomed.": Haisten, "OSU 41, Nebraska 29."

57    We knew (the Cowboys) were a great second-half team.: Haisten, "OSU 41, Nebraska 29."

58    Bob Stoops started the talk . . . tie at the top.": Allen and Gundy, pp. 232, 234.

58    When the Sooners gathered . . . toward the OSU fans.: Allen and Gundy, p. 238.

58    about a dozen Sooners . . . back to the bench area.: Allen and Gundy, p. 241.

58    the Cowboys "put the . . . of roughly eight minutes.: Allen and Gundy, p. 241.

58    "the locker room was the . . . their championship trophy.: Allen and Gundy, p. 242.

58    All week I said . . . because of you guys.': Allen and Gundy, p. 242.

59    "One of the most entertaining games of the 1987-88 bowl season": "1987 Sun Bowl," *Wikipedia, the free encyclopedia*, http://en.wikipedia.org/wiki/1987_Sun_Bowl.

59    He would start his next . . . his heart wasn't in it.: Jimmie Tramel, "All-Oklahoma All-Bowl Team," *Tulsa World*, Dec. 17, 2006, http://www.tulsaworld.com/article.aspx/All_ Oklahoma_All_Bowl_Team_The_Best_of_the_Bowls/061217_Sp_B1_Besto10794.

59    That was my 15 seconds of fame.: Tramel, "All-Oklahoma All-Bowl Team."

60    On a golf course in 1957, . . . to their exclusive club.: Bischoff, *Mr. Iba*, p. 197.

60    They determined that OSU . . . basketball play in 1959.: Bischoff, *Mr. Iba*, p. 198.

60    Iba hoped that the . . . season as an independent.: Bischoff, *Mr. Iba*, p. 199.

60    Arlen Clark, a natural forward . . . other starter exceeded six feet,: Bischoff, *Mr. Iba*, p. 199.

60    the Wildcat coach asked Iba . . . and we must be friends.": Bischoff, *Mr. Iba*, p. 200.

61    "I thought if I worked . . . field goals or whatever.": Jason Elmquist, "Oklahoma State Kicker Dan Bailey Exceeds Expectations," *Stillwater NewsPress*, Dec. 28, 2010, http://stwnews press.com/osusports/x480667653.

61    "I just remember turning . . . he expects to make it,": Terry Tush, "Bailey's Kick Saves Cowboys," *GoPokes*, Sept. 30, 2010, http://oklahomastate.scout.com/2/1007731.html.

61    To play four years . . . expectations I had.: Elmquist, "Oklahoma State Kicker Dan Bailey."

62    Rader was clearly . . . OSU's senior tailback: John Klein, "Rader's Worst Nightmare Occurred: Thompson," *Tulsa World*, Sept. 15, 1996, http://www.tulsaworld.com/ article.aspx/Raders_Worst_Nightmare_Occurred_Thompson/19960915_Sp_b1klein.

62    Five years before, he had . . . back in the state.: Jimmie Tramel, "Rader Baffled by Thompson," *Tulsa World*, Sept. 16, 1996, http://www.tulsaworld.com/article.aspx/Rader_ Baffled_By_Thompson/19960916_Sp_b1rader.

62    Rader let his safeties . . . the half" to Thompson.": Tramel, "Rader Baffled by Thompson."

62    the tenth-best rushing day . . . against Missouri in 1990.: Dan O'Kane, "Thompson: Real Stars Fill Line," *Tulsa World*, Sept. 15, 1996, http://tulsaworld.com/article/aspx/ Thompson_Real_Stars_Fill_Line_Hole_Was_There_Every_Time/584090.

62    "How did they do that?" . . . "Thompson had a great game,": Tramel, "Rader Baffled."

62    Dave Rader's worst nightmare . . . the Lewis field turf.: Klein, "Rader's Worst Nightmare."

63    Not long after his football . . . starting center Evan Epstein.: Kelly Hines, "Heart of Dallas Bowl Has Special Meaning to Former OSU Player John Corker," *Tulsa World*, Jan. 2, 2013, http://www.tulsaworld.com/article.aspx/Heart_of_Dallas_Bowl_has_special_

**194**

meaning_to_former_OSU_player_John_Corker/20130102_93_B7_CUTLIN999200.

63    The Lord has made me . . . productive in society again.: Hines, "Heart of Dallas Bowl Has Special Meaning."

64    The officials are the authority on the court.: Bill Haisten, "Oklahoma State Downs Seminoles, Makes It to Sweet Sixteen," *Tulsa World*, March 24, 2008, http://www.tulsaworld. com/article.aspx/Oklahoma_State_downs_Seminoles_makes_it_to_Sweet_Sixteen/ 20080324_2_DESMO44424.

65    Knauls was not highly recruited, . . . land him a scholarship.: Jimmie Tramel, "Attention-Grabber." *Tulsa World*, Aug. 22, 1999, http://www.tulsaworld.com/article.aspx/ Attention_grabber/1990821_co_TABBATT.

65    I knew that my heart . . . with the best of them.: Tramel, "Attention-Grabber."

66    "Football is a violent . . . a certain measure of courage.": Bill Haisten, "O-State's Coe Has Endured a Litany of Setbacks," *Tulsa World*, Sept. 19, 2007, http://www.tulsaworld. com/article.aspx/O_States_Coe_has_endured_a_litany_of_setbacks/070919_2_B1_ ENWor43002.

66    Coe suffered "a litany of . . . express their respect for him.: Haisten, "O-State's Coe."

66    "I feel like God puts . . . takes the easy way out.": Haisten, "O-State's Coe."

66    By anyone's definition, Clint Coe is courageous and tough.: Haisten, "O-State's Coe."

67    To even warm up . . . instead of female anatomy.": Jones with Tramel, *Pat Jones' Tales*, p. 166.

67    the Grambling band wound . . . for a first down.: Jones with Tramel, *Pat Jones' Tales*, p. 167.

67    It was tough to set . . . going on around us.: Jones with Tramel, *Pat Jones' Tales*, p. 166.

68    their head coach described as "a total meltdown.": Bill Haisten, "Rout 66: OSU Wins," *Tulsa World*, Nov. 12, 2006, http://www.tulsaworld.com/article.aspx/Rout_66_OSU_ wins/061112_Sp_B1_Rout624902.

68    his first carry of the season.: Hairston, "Rout 66."

68    Bedford had promised his players . . . by at least 18 points.: Bill Haisten, "Notebook: Bedford Keeps Promise," *Tulsa World*, Nov. 12, 2006, http://www.tulsaworld.com/article. aspx/Notebook_Bedford_keeps_promise/061112_Sp_B5_OSUBa23102.

68    Bedford arrived in . . . cutting my hair off.": Haisten, "Notebook: Bedford Keeps Promise."

68    I'm too old to have . . . might not grow back.: Haisten, "Notebook: Bedford Keeps Promise."

69    As Gearhart learned the game, . . . "She refuses to move,": John Helsley, "OSU's Mariah Gearhart Stands Her Ground," *NewsOK.com*, May 10, 2011, newsok.com/osus-mariah-gearhart-stands-her-ground/article/3566701.

69    "I've had some bruises . . . but I really do,": Helsley, "OSU's Mariah Gearhart."

69    The 60 feet going from . . . to go away for me.: Helsley, "OSU's Mariah Gearhart."

70    Only eight seniors and a . . . up for the first game.: Jones with Tramel, *Pat Jones' Tales*, p. 7.

70    A strong of injuries . . . freshmen or walk-ons.: Jones with Tramel, *Pat Jones' Tales*, p. 16.

70    "the ball bounced our . . . made our own breaks.": Jones with Tramel, *Pat Jones' Tales*, p. 17.

70    "If they had punted, . . . they got us, they got us,": Jones with Tramel, *Pat Jones' Tales*, p. 17.

70    Colorado ran a quarterback . . . to stop him short.: Jones with Tramel, *Pat Jones' Tales*, p. 18.

70    Jones called the 21-20 win the "Miracle in the Rockies.": Jones with Tramel, *Pat Jones' Tales*, p. 18.

71    Shaw was at his healthiest. He "came off the bench in style,": Mike Brown, "Shaw Symbol of Cowboy Depth," *Tulsa World*, Nov. 21, 2004, http://www.tulsaworld.com/article.aspx/ Shaw_symbol_of_Cowboy_depth/041121/Sp_B3_Shaws442.

71    "They just mashed us up front,": Bill Haisten, "Shaw Fills in as Cowboys Rush to Win," *Tulsa World*, Nov. 14, 2004, http://www.tulsaworld.com/article.aspx/Shaw_fills_in_as_ Cowboys_rush_to_win/041114_Sp_B1_Shaw47658.

72    Athletic Director Myron Roderick . . . pouring it down her backside.": Rhett Morgan, "For Chills, OSU-OU Has Had Its Share," *Tulsa World*, Oct. 23, 1998, http://www.tulsa-world.com/articles.aspx/For_chills_OSU_OU_has_had_its_share/L102398029.

72    That's the way it happend. It's pretty unusual.: Morgan, "For Chills."

73    The win ended the Jayhawks' . . . a top-5 team on the road.: "Cowboys Knock Off No. 2 Jayhawks on the Road," *Stillwater NewsPress*, Feb. 2, 2013, http://www.stnews press.com/highschoolsports/x1303538130.

73    "in one of the rare . . . to hold things together.": "Cowboys Knock Off No. 2 Jayhawks."

73    scored seven of his . . . the game's final minutes.: "Cowboys Knock Off No. 2 Jayhawks."
73    Brown let out a roar, . . . combination on the court.: "Cowboys Knock Off No. 2 Jayhawks."
73    I was so ecstatic . . . just came to me to do it.: "Cowboys Knock Off No. 2 Jayhawks."
74    "We go through these scenarios all the time,": Matt Doyle, "Practice Pays Off for OSU,"
       *Tulsa World*, Oct. 21, 2007, http://www.tulsaworld.com/article.aspx/Practice_pays_
       pays_off_for_OSU_on_last_drive/071021_2_B7_hrbri25774.
74    that pass play was one . . . to making that catch,": Doyle, "Practice Pays Off for OSU."
74    There's [no] doubt these .. . confidence in that situation.: Doyle, "Practice Pays Off for OSU."
75    There he met Julie . . . all I will say here,": Jimmie Tramel, " Oklahoma State's New Offen-
       sive Coordinator, Mike Yurcich, Is a Virtual Puzzle to Fans," *Tulsa World*, Aug. 25,
       2013, http://www.tulsaworld.com/article.aspx/Oklahoma_States?new_offensive_
       coordinator_Mike_Yurcich_is_a_virtual_puzzle_to_fans/20130825_93_B1_CUTLIN
       976237.
75    From his first step, . . . and spend time together.': Jimmie Tramel, "Oklahoma State's New
       Offensive Coordinator."
76    In the 1920s and '30s, . . . and the match resumed: Palmer, "Ed Gallagher."
76    Outfitted in Stetson hats, . . . whenever they traveled.: Palmer, "Ed Gallagher."
77    The top ten list is taken from "Ten Greatest Oklahoma State Cowboys," at *AthlonSports.com*/
       college-football/slideshow/top-ten-greatest-oklahoma-state-cowboys.
77    "is arguably the most productive receiver in program history.": "Ten Greatest Oklahoma
       State Cowboys."
78    "We started dinking and dunking,": Jones with Tramel, *Pat Jones' Tales*, p. 89.
78    The coaches immediately . . . and stop the clock.: Jones with Tramel, *Pat Jones' Tales*, p. 89.
78    Hanna "brutally drove [the ball] . . . more Gamecocks hanging on": Pat Quinn, "Cowboy
       Football: Hanna Etches His Name in Cowboy Football Lore," *okstate.com*, Nov. 16,
       2010, http://www.okstate.com/sports-m-footbl-spec-rel/111610aah.html.
79    Jones was such a charismatic . . . to host recruits on campus.: Jimmie Tramel, "OSU's
       Richetti Jones Can Walk, Talk a Good Game," *Tulsa World*, Nov. 10, 2011, http://
       www.tulsaworld.com/article.aspx.OSUs_Richetti_Jones_can_walk_talk_a_good_
       game/20111110_93_B1_CUTLIN21872.
79    "I am like, 'yes, . . . out it was an earthquake.: Jimmie Tramel, "OSU's Richetti Jones."
79    When the stadium began . . . he told them so.: Jimmie Tramel, "OSU's Richetti Jones."
79    When I got home and . . . an I-told-you-so face.": Jimmie Tramel, "OSU's Richetti Jones."
80    Four surgeries in seven years . . . kind of knees that I have,": Marquette Martin, "Megan
       Byford of Oklahoma State Perseveres," *BleacherReport.com*, March 15, 2010, http://
       bleacherreport.com/articles/363241.
80    playing on with the . . . starter in the Big 12.": Martin, "Megan Byford of Oklahoma State."
80    "I love basketball," . . . he's really been good to me," Martin, "Megan Byford of Oklahoma
       State."
80    For what she can give . . . day on [the] floor.": Martin, "Megan Byford of Oklahoma State."
81    only one week after OSU . . . right into Brown's hands.: Jimmie Tramel, "Cowboys Tech-led
       to Death," *Tulsa World*, Oct. 10, 1999, http://www.tulsaworld.com/article.aspx/
       Cowboys_Tech_led_to_death/L101099085.
81    "millions of crickets rained down . . . which started at 11:30 a.m.: Ralph W. Marler, "Crickets
       'Everywhere,'" *Tulsa World*, Oct. 13, 1999, http://www.tulsaworld.com/article.aspx/
       Crickets_everywhere/19991013_Ne_a9crick.
81    We were picking them . . . the (press box) window.": Marler, "Crickets 'Everywhere.'"
82    "basketball-on-grass" offense: John E. Hoover, "Miles Will Stick with Game Plan," *Tulsa
       World*, Oct. 16, 2003, http://www.tulsaworld.com/article.aspx/Miles_will_stick_with_
       game_plan/031016_Sp_b9_miles.
82    The machine that had . . . in a frenzied fourth quarter: Matt Doyle, "Holding out for a
       Hero," *Tulsa World*, Oct. 19, 2003, http://www.tulsaworld.com/article.aspx/Holding_
       out_for_a_hero/ 031019_Sp_b7_holding.
82    Right before I went . . . had to make a play.: Doyle, "Holding out for a Hero."
83    "I played some flag football . . . were on the team.: John Helsley, "Oklahoma State's Taylor
       Sokolosky Finds His Calling Is Football," *NewsOK.com*, Oct. 1, 2009, http://newsok.
       com/oklahoma-states-taylor-sokolosky-finds-his-calling-is-football/article/340529.

**196**

83   "an elite private school known . . . concentrate on special teams.: Helsley, "Oklahoma State's
     Taylor Sokolosky."
83   The team was practicing kickoff . . . starting kickoff coverage team.": Matt Doyle, "Soko-
     losky Earns Sport," *Tulsa World*, Oct. 17, 2007, http://www.tulsaworld.com/article.
     aspx/Sokolosky_earns_spot/071017_2_B6_hrbri18843.
83   I didn't feel I . . . college [and] keep playing.: Helsley, "Oklahoma State's Taylor Sokolosky."
84   In a pickup game before . . . What's the shame in either?": "Home on the Range," *Sports
     Illustrated*, Nov. 29, 1993, http://sportsillustrated.cnn.com/vault/article/magazine/
     MAG1138287/index.htm.
84   I like the name. It fits.: "Home on the Range."
85   He called a staff meeting . . . The deal was done.: Jones with Tramel, *Pat Jones' Tales*, p. 65.
85   Jones left and went to . . . knocking on the door.: Jones with Tramel, *Pat Jones' Tales*, p. 66.
85   He wasn't sure how . . . "but I trusted him.": Jones with Tramel, *Pat Jones' Tales*, p. 65.
85   Iba had some twofold . . . wielding his enormous clout.: Jones with Tramel, *Pat Jones' Tales*,
     p. 66.
85   Jones later talked for . . . Jones answered, "Yes, sir.": Jones with Tramel, *Pat Jones' Tales*, p. 67.
85   Of every living being . . . Iba was Oklahoma State.: Jones with Tramel, *Pat Jones' Tales*, p. 66.
86   "what had to be one of . . . status this entire season.": Scott Nulph, "Third-Stringer Saves
     Cowboys' Season," *Stillwater NewsPress*, Nov. 20, 2009, http://www.stwnewspress.
     com/osusports/x546372780.
86   he had to run out . . . fun to get out there.": Justin Hite, "Wonderful Weeden," *Stillwater
     NewsPress*, Nov. 20, 2009, http://www.stwnewspress.com/osusports/x546372782.
86   Surprised may be the . . . been out there enough.: Hite, "Wonderful Weeden."
87   Sanders would have to . . . big linemen into cabs.: Jones with Tramel, *Pat Jones' Tales*, p. 164.
87   He also told the TV . . . "and we got out of there.": Jones with Tramel, *Pat Jones' Tales*, p. 165.
87   It was a big deal . . . Trophy winner present.: Jones with Tramel, *Pat Jones' Tales*, p. 165.
88   So had they been, . . .teammates called[ed] him Gumby.": Bruce Anderson, "At Last a Title
     for the Cowboys," *Sports Illustrated*, March 27, 1989, http://sportsillustrated.cnn.com/
     vault/article/magazine/MAG1126664.
88   He trailed 8-7 with time . . . waving to the Iowa fans.: Anderson, "At Last a Title."
88   By the time Cross . . . won the team championship.: Anderson, "At Last a Title."
88   Never's a long time. I guess 'never' is today.: Anderson, "At Last a Title."
89   A five-star recruit rated as . . . our position in recruiting.": Bill Haisten, "Big Man, Big
     Impact," *Tulsa World*, Dec. 27, 2006, http://www.tulsaworld.com/article.aspx/Big_
     man_big_impact/061227_Sp_B4_Bigma6036.
89   "He couldn't control his . . . to do on the field.": Haisten, "Big Man, Big Impact."
89   He never misses a class . . . he'll very successful.": Haisten, "Big Man, Big Impact."
90   "old cement bunker of a dressing room.": Allen and Gundy, p. 124.
90   The initial estimate was that . . . stalled right over the stadium.: Allen and Gundy, p. 122.
90   The team's pre-game meal had . . . into a makeshift kitchen.: Allen and Gundy, p. 131.
90   cutting off the crust for . . . he was allergic to peanuts.: Allen and Gundy, p. 132.
90   We had peanut butter and . . . as fast as we could.: Allen and Gundy, p. 132.
91   Les Miles once said he fit right in with Thurman Thomas and Barry Sanders.: John E.
     Hoover, "Tailback U. Started with Fenimore," *Tulsa World*, Sept. 12, 2003, http://www.
     tulsaworld.com/article.aspx/Tailback_U_started_with_Fenimore/030912?Sp_b1_tail.
91   "fold-up helmets, no face masks and minimal padding.": Hoover, "Tailback U. Started with
     Fenimore."
91   During the week of . . . called off the starters.: Hoover, "Tailback U. Started with Fenimore."
91   We decided we were . . . to beat them 55-0.: Hoover, "Tailback U. Started with Fenimore."
92   It was the 108th straight . . . go out with a bang.": Bill Haisten, "Bittersweet Farewell," *Tulsa
     World*, 23 Nov. 2007, http://www.tulsaworld.com/article.aspx/Bittersweet_farewell/
     071123_238_B1_hForn37824.
92   It is a good way to end it.: Bill Haisten, "Finishing in Style," *Tulsa World*, Jan. 1, 2008, http://
     www.tulsaworld.com/article.aspx/Finishing_in_style/080101_2_B1_ENWor
     28180.

# BIBLIOGRAPHY

Allen, Robert and Mike Gundy. *More Than a Championship: The 2011 Oklahoma State Cowboys*. Oklahoma City: Oklahoma Heritage Association, 2012.

Anderson, Bruce. "At Last a Title for the Cowboys." *Sports Illustrated*. 27 March 1989. http://sportsillustrated.cnn.com/vault/article/magazine/MAG1126664/index.htm.

Beech, Mark. "State Secret." *Sports Illustrated*. 18 Oct. 2004. http://sportsillustrated.cnn.com/vault/article/magazine/MAG1113275/index.htm.

Bischoff, John Paul. *Mr. Iba: Basketball's Aggie Iron Duke*. Oklahoma City: Oklahoma Heritage Association, 1980.

Blockus, Gary R. "Jordan Oliver Seeks Second NCAA Wrestling Championship." *The Morning Call*. 19 March 2013. http://articles.mcall.com/2013-03-19/sports/mc-oliver-wrestling-nationals-03192013-2013.

"Bob Fenimore, All-American at OSU, Dies at Age 84." *Tulsa World*. 28 July 2010. http://www.tulsaworld.com/article.aspx/Bob_Fenimore_All_American_at_OSU_dies_at_age_84/20100728_93_0_bobfen873290.

Brown, Mike. "Running Directly at Their Challenge." *Tulsa World*. 24 Oct. 2004. http://www.tulsaworld.com/article.aspx/Running_directly_at_their_challenge/041024/Sp_B7_Runni3657.

-----. "Shaw Symbol of Cowboy Depth." *Tulsa World*. 21 Nov. 2004. http://tulsaworld.com/article.aspx/Shaw_symbol_of_Cowboy_depth/041121/Sp_B3_Shaws442.

Buchanan, Olin. "Blackmon Making a Name for Himself." *rivals.com*. 5 May 2011. http://collegefootball.rivals.com/content.asp?CID=1218606.

Carlson, Jenni. "Former OSU Football Coach Jim Stanley Dies." *NewsOK.com*. 12 Jan. 2012. newsok.com/former-osu-football-coach-jim-stanley-dies/article/3639689.

Chen, Albert. "Uprising in Stillwater." *Sports Illustrated*. 14 Sept. 2009. http://sportsillustrated.cnn.com/vault/article/magazine/MAG 1160023/index.htm.

"Cowboy Football: Remembering a Cowboy Legend." *okstate.com*. 8 Sept. 2010. http://www.okstate.com/sports/m-footbl/spec-rel/090810aab.html.

"Cowboy Wrestling: Dynasty Defined." *okstate.com*. http://www.okstate.com/sports/m-wrestl/spec-rel/wr-tradition.html.

"Cowboys Knock Off No. 2 Jayhawks on the Road." *Stillwater NewsPress*. 2 Feb. 2013. http://www.stwnewspress.com/highschoolsports/x1303538130.

Culpepper, R. Alan. "The Gospel of Luke: Introduction, Commentary, and Reflections." *The New Interpreter's Bible*. Vol. IX. Nashville: Abingdon Press, 1998. pp. 1-490.

Day, Chris. "Oklahoma State Fullback Kye Staley Finally Gets His Touchdown." *Stillwater NewsPress*. 30 Oct. 2011. http://www.stwnewspress.com/osusports/x783647696.

Doyle, Matt. "Cowboys Add a Trick to the Kick." *Tulsa World*. 12 Oct. 2003. http://www.tulsaworld.com/article.aspx/Cowboys_add_a_trick_to_the_kick/031012_Sp_b6_cow.

-----. "Final Defensive Play Saves Cowboys." *Tulsa World*. 23 Sept. 2007. http://www.tulsaworld.com/article.aspx/Final_defensive_play_saves_Cowboys/070923_Z_B19_hrbri10720.

-----. "Holding out for a Hero." *Tulsa World*. 19 Oct. 2003. http://www.tulsaworld.com/article.aspx/Holding_out_for_a_hero/031019_Sp_b7_holding.

-----. "Practice Pays Off for OSU on Last Drive." *Tulsa World*. 21 Oct. 2007. http://www.tulsaworld.com/article.aspx/Practice_pays_off_for_OSU_on_last-drive/071021_2_B7_hrbri25774.

-----. "Sokolosky Earns Spot." *Tulsa World*. 17 Oct. 2007. http://www.tulsaworld.com/article.axpx/Sokolosky_earns_spot/071017_2_B6_hrbri18843.

Elmquist, Jason. "Oklahoma State Football Finds Ways to Have Fun." *Stillwater NewsPress*. 28 Dec. 2012. http://www.stwnewspress.com/osusports/x503807920.

-----. "Oklahoma State Kicker Dan Bailey Exceeds Expectations." *Stillwater NewsPress*. 28

Dec. 2010. http://www.stwnewspress.com/osusports/x480667653.

-----. "Oliver's Win Cements Wrestling Legacy at OSU." *Stillwater NewsPress*. 26 March 2013. http://www.stwnewspress.com/osusports/x149931924.

Garrity, John. "They're Runnin' and Gunnin'." *Sports Illustrated*. 16 Feb. 1981. http://www.sportsillustrated.cnn.com/vault/article/magazine/MAG1124223/index.htm.

Greene, Dan. "Southwest Success Story." *Sports Illustrated*. 12 Aug. 2011. http://sports illustrated.cnn.com/vault/article/magazine/MAG1188655/index.htm.

Haisten, Bill. "A House United." *Tulsa World*. 22 Nov. 2007. http://www.tulsaworld.com/article.aspx/A_house_united/071122_238_B1_hThef11578.

-----. "Big Man, Big Impact." *Tulsa World*. 27 Dec. 2006. http://www.tulsaworld.com/article.aspx/Big_man_big_impact/061227_Sp_B4_Bigma6036.

-----. "Bittersweet Farewell." *Tulsa World*. 23 Nov. 2007. http://www.tulsaworld.com/article.aspx/Bittersweet_farewell/071123_238_B1_hForn37824.

-----. "Bobby Reid's Evolution." *Tulsa World*. 17 Oct. 2006. http://www.tulsaworld.com/article.aspx/Bobby_Reids_evolution/061017_Sp_B1_QBflo3835.

-----. "Comeback Cowboy." *Tulsa World*. 29 Aug. 2008, http://www.tulsaworld.com/article.aspx/Comeback_Cowboy/20080829_93_B1_OSUwid878851.

-----. "Fine Finale." *Tulsa World*. 29 Dec. 2006. http://www.tulsaworld.com/article.aspx/Fine_finale/061229_Sp_B1_Lated28541.

-----. "Finishing in Style." *Tulsa World*. 1 Jan. 2008. http://www.tulsaworld.com/article.aspx/Finishing_in_style/08001_2_B1_ENWor28180.

-----. "How They Scored." *Tulsa World*. 14 Oct. 2007. http://www.tulsaworld.com/article.aspx/How_They_Scored/071014_2_B16_hrbri640.

-----. "Notebook: Bedford Keeps Promise." *Tulsa World*. 12 Nov. 2006. http://www.tulsa world.com/article.aspx/Notebook_Bedford_keeps_promise/061112_Sp_B5_OSUBa23102.

-----. "Oklahoma State Downs Seminoles, Makes It to Sweet Sixteen." *Tulsa World*. 24 March 2008. http://www.tulsaworld.com/article.aspx/Oklahoma_State_downs_Seminoles_makes_it_to_Sweet_Sixteen/20080324_2_DESMO44424.

-----. "O-State's Coe Has Endured a Litany of Setbacks." *Tulsa World*. 19 Sept. 2007. http://www.tulsaworld.com/article.aspx/O_States_Coe_has_endured_a_litany_of_setbacks/070919_2_B1_ENWor43002.

-----. "OSU 41, Nebraska 29: OSU Pops Corn." *Tulsa World*. 29 Oct. 2006. http://www.tulsa world.com/article.aspx/OSU_41_Nebraska_29_OSU_pops_corn/061029_Sp_B11_OSUov28266.

-----. "OSU Kicks Back." *Tulsa World*. 24 Oct. 2004. http://www.tulsaworld.com/article.aspx/OSU_kicks_back/041024_Sp_B7_OSUki55637.

-----. "OSU Tops Tech." *Tulsa World*. 23 Sept. 2007. http://www.tulsaworld.com/article.aspx/OSU_tops_Tech/070923_Z_B11_ENWor78485.

-----. "Rout 66: OSU Wins." *Tulsa World*. 12 Nov. 2006. http://www.tulsaworld.com/Rout_66_OSU_wins/061112_Sp_B1_Rout624902.

-----. "Shaw Fills in as Cowboys Rush to Win." *Tulsa World*. 14 Nov. 2004. http://tulsa world.com/article.aspx/Shaw_fills_in_as_Cowboys_rush_to_win/041114_Sp_B1_Shaw47658.

-----. "Updated: Oklahoma State Blows Out Nebraska 45-14." *Tulsa World*. 13 Oct. 2007. http://www.tulsaworld.com/article/aspx/Updated_Oklahoma_State_blows_out_Nebraska_45_14/071013_2_LINCO85470.

Helsley, John. "Oklahoma State's Taylor Sokolosky Finds His Calling Is Football." *NewsOK. com*. 1 Oct. 2009. http://newsok.com/oklahoma-states-taylor-sokolosky-finds-his-calling-is-football/article/340529.

-----. "OSU's Mariah Gearhart Stands Her Ground." *NewsOK.com*. 10 May 2011. http://newsok.com/osus-mariah-gearhart-stands-her-ground/article/3566701.

Hines, Kelly. "Heart of Dallas Bowl Has Special Meaning to Former OSU Player John Corker." *Tulsa World*. 2 Jan. 2013. http://www.tulsaworld.com/article.aspx/Heart_ of_Dallas_Bowl_has_special_meaning_to_former_OSU_player_John_Corker/ 20130202_93_B7_CUTLIN999200.

Hite, Justin. "Wonderful Weeden." *Stillwater NewsPress*. 20 Nov. 2009. http://www.stw newspress.com/osusports/x546372782.

"Home on the Range." *Sports Illustrated*. 29 Nov. 1993. http://sportsillustrated.cnn.com/ vault/article/magazine/MAG1138287/index.htm.

Hoover, John E. "97th Bedlam Battle: It's No Fluke." *Tulsa World*. 1 Dec. 2002.http://tulsa world.com/article.aspx/97th_Bedlam_Battle_Its_no_Fluke/021201_Sp_B1_itsno.

-----. "Back in the Saddle." *Tulsa World*. 2 March 2004. http://www.tulsaworld.com/article. aspx/Back_in_the_Saddle/Sp_b1_back.

-----. "Bell's Long Smile Tops 1,000 Yards." *Tulsa World*. 28 Dec. 2002. http://www.tulsa world.com/article.aspx/Bells_long_smile_tops_1000_yards/021228_Sp_89_bells.

-----. "Coronation Day." *Tulsa World*. 7 March 2004. http://www.tulsaworld.com/article. aspx/Coronation_day/040307_Sp_b1_coron.

-----. "Having a Fields Day." *Tulsa World*. 17 Nov. 2002. http://www.tulsaworld.com/article. aspx/Having_a_Fields_day/021117_Sp_B1_Havin.

-----. "Howell Shines in Rare Chance." *Tulsa World*. 9 Nov. 1997. http://www.tulsaworld. com/article.aspx/Howell_Shines_in_Rare_Chance/19971108.

-----. "Miles' Decision Avoids Close Call." *Tulsa World*. 8 Sept. 2003. http://www.tulsaworld. com/article.aspx/Miles_decision_avoids_close_call/030908_Sp_b8_miles.

-----. "Miles Will Stick with Game Plan." *Tulsa World*. 16 Oct. 2003. http://www.tulsaworld. com/article.aspx/Miles_will_stick_with_game_plan/031016_S p_b9_miles.

-----. "Right Back on Track." *Tulsa World*. 12 Oct. 2003. http://www.tulsaworld.com/article. aspx/Right_back_on_track/031012_Sp_b1_right.

-----. "Tailback U. Started with Fenimore." *Tulsa World*. 12 Sept. 2003. http://www.tulsa world.com/article.aspx/Tailback_U_started_with_Fenimore/030912_Sp_b1_tail.

Jones, Pat with Jimmie Tramel. *Pat Jones' Tales from Oklahoma State Football*. Champaign, Ill.: Sports Publishing L.L.C., 2007.

Kirshenbaum, Jerry, ed. "They Said It." *Sports Illustrated*. 8 Oct. 1984. http://sports illustrated.cnn.com/vault/article/magazine/MAG1122687/index.htm.

Klein, John. "20 Years Ago, Aggie Defense Was Destroyed." *Tulsa World*. 3 Oct. 2008. www. tulsaworld.com/article.aspx/20_years_ago_Aggie_defense_was_destroyed/ 20081003_203_b1_BARRYS473786.

-----. "Bedlam Became a Shocker." *Tulsa World*. 25 Nov. 2001. http://www.tulsaworld.com/ article.aspx/Bedlam_became_a_shocker/L112501097.

-----. "Cowboys Cap Season with Thriller." *Tulsa World*. 29 Dec. 2006. http://www.tulsa world.com/article.aspx/Cowboys_cap_season_with_thriller/061299_Sp_B1_ Cowbo9042.

-----. "Cowboys Change Direction." *Tulsa World*. 24 Oct. 2004. http://www.tulsaworld.com/ article.aspx/Cowboys_change_direction/041024_Sp_B6_Cowboy36122.

-----. "James Wadley Looking Forward to the View from the Stands." *Tulsa World*. 3 May 2012. www.tulsaworld.com/article.aspx/John_Klein_James_Wadley_looking_ forward_to_the_view_from_the_stands/20120503_203_b1_jamesw41659.

-----. "OSU Salts Wound." *Tulsa World*. 1 Dec. 2002. http://www.tulsaworld.com/article. aspx/OSU_salts_wound/021201_Ne_a1_twice.

-----. "Rader's Worst Nightmare Occurred: Thompson." *Tulsa World*. 15 Sept. 1996. http:// www.tulsaworld.com/article.aspx/Raders_Worst_Nightmare_Occurred_Thomp-son/19960915_Sp_b1klein.

Lipsey, Rick. "Down to the Wire." *Sports Illustrated*. 12 June 1995. http://sportsillustrated. cnn.com/vault/article/magazine/MAG1006704/index.htm.

MacArthur, John. *Twelve Ordinary Men*. Nashville: W Publishing Group, 2002.

Marler, Ralph W. "Crickets 'Everywhere.'" *Tulsa World*. 13 Oct. 1999. http://www.tulsa world.com/article/Crickets_everywhere/19991013_Ne_a9crick.

Martin, Marquette. "Megan Byford of Oklahoma State Perseveres for Love of the Game." *BleacherReport.com*. 15 March 2010. http://bleacherreport.com/articles/363241.

McDermott, Barry. "A Wake for Wake Forest." *Sports Illustrated*. 21 June 1976. http://sports illustrated.cnn.com/vault/article/magazine/MAG1091235/index.htm.

Mizell, Gina. "Oklahoma State Women's Basketball: 2008 Bedlam Win Turned the Tide for Cowgirls Basketball." *NewsOK.com*. 22 Feb. 2013. http://newsok.com/oklahoma-state-womens-basketball-2008-bedlam-win-turned-the-tide-for-cowgirls-basketball/article/3758229.

Morgan, Rhett. "Cowboys Get Mile-High Lift." *Tulsa World*. 12 Oct. 1997. http://www.tulsa world.com/articles.aspx/Cowboys_Get_Mile_High_Lift_Lindsay_Mayes_TD_Pass_Reels/634784.

-----. "For Chills, OSU-OU Has Had Its Share." *Tulsa World*. 23 Oct. 1998. http://www.tulsa world.com/articles.aspx/For_chills_OSU_OU_has_had_its_share/L102398029.

-----. "It's an Orange-Letter Day: Cowboys Swamp Sooners With Historic Victory." *Tulsa World*. 9 Nov. 1997. http://www.tulsaworld.com/article/aspx/Its_an_Orange_Letter_Day_Cowboys_Swamp_Sooners_With_Historic_Victory/638532.

Mule, Marty. "How Oklahoma A&M and St. Mary's Met in the 1946 Sugar Bowl." from *Sugar Bowl Classic: A History*. reprinted at http://allstatesugarbowl.org/site155.php.

Munn, Scott. "State College Notebook: Former OSU Wide Receiver Artrell Woods at UCO." *NewsOK.com*. 4 Aug. 2010. http://newsok.com/state-college-notebook-former-osu-wide-receiver-artrell-woods-at-uco/article/3482389.

Murphy, Austin. "Slick and Oh-So Quick." *Sports Illustrated*. 22 March 1999. http://sports illustrated.cnn.com/vault/article/magazine/MAG1015361/index.htm.

Neff, Craig. "The Importance of Ernest." *Sports Illustrated*. 25 Oct. 1982. http://sports illustrated.cnn.com/vault/article/magazine/MAG1126040/index.htm.

Nulph, Scott. "Third-Stringer Saves Cowboys' Season." *Stillwater NewsPress*. 20 Nov. 2009. http://www.stwnewspress.com/osusports/x546372780.

O'Kane, Dan. "OU KO'd." *Tulsa World*. 25 Nov. 2001. http://www.tulsaworld.com/article.aspx/OU_KOd/L112501098.

-----. "Thompson: Real Stars Fill Line; Hole Was 'There Every Time.'" *Tulsa World*. 15 Sept. 1996. http://www.tulsaworld.com/article.aspx/Thompson_Real_Stars_Fill_Line_Hole_Was_There_Every_Time/584090.

"Oklahoma State Cowboys Wrestling." *Wikipedia, the free encyclopedia*. http://en.wikipedia.org/wiki/Oklahoma_State_Cowboys_wrestling.

Palmer, Mark. "Ed Gallagher: Father of Intercollegiate Wrestling." *revwrestling.com*. 31 July 2008. Reprinted at *okstate.com*. http://www.okstate.com/sports/m-wrestl/spec-rel/wr-tradition.html.

Price, S.L. "The Gift." *Sports Illustrated*. 6 July 1998. http://sportsillustrated.cnn.com/vault/article/magazine/MAG1012190/index.htm.

Quinn, Pat. "Cowboy Football: Hanna Etches His Name in Cowboy Football Lore." *okstate.com*. 16 Nov. 2010. http://www.okstate.com/sports/m-footbl/spec-rel/111610aah.html.

Reed. William F. "Rough and Ready." *Sports Illustrated*. 11 March 1991. http://sports illustrated.cnn.com/vault/article/magazine/MAG 1118947/index.htm.

Schroeder, George. "At Oklahoma State, The Student Became the Teacher This Spring." *SI.com*. 15 April 2011. http://sportsillustrated.cnn.com/2011/writers/george_schroeder/04/14/

Shelton, Christopher. "OSU Athletes Reveal Unique Habits." *Stillwater NewsPress*. 6 June 2009. http://www.stwnewspress.com/osusports/x681627934.

Sittler, Dave. "OSU Will Remember Nov. 24, 2001." *Tulsa World*. 25 Nov. 2001. http://www.tulsaworld.com/article.aspx/OSU_will_remember_

Nov_24_2001/L112501067.

"Ten Greatest Oklahoma State Cowboys." *AthlonSports.com*. athlonsports.com/college-football/slideshow/top-ten-greatest-oklahoma-state-cowboys.

Tramel, Berry. "Tennis Coach James Wadley is OSU's Grand Old Man."*NewsOK.com*. 27 Sept. 2009. newsok.com/tennis-coach-james-wadley-is-osus-grand-old-man/article/3404086.

Tramel, Jimmie. "All-Oklahoma All-Bowl Team: The Best of the Bowls." *Tulsa World*. 17 Dec. 2006. http://www.tulsaworld.com/article.aspx/All_Oklahoma_All_Bowl_Team_The_Best_of_the_Bowls/061217_Sp_B1_Besto10794.

-----. "Attention-Gabber." *Tulsa World*. 22 Aug. 1999. http://www.tulsaworld.com/article.aspx/Attention_grabber/1990821_co_TABBATT.

-----. "Country Boy at Heart." *Tulsa World*. 6 Nov. 2001. http://www.tulsaworld.com/article.aspx/Country_boy_at_heart/1011105_Sp_b1woods.

-----. "Cowboys Tick-led to Death." *Tulsa World*. 10 Oct. 1999. http://www.tulsaworld.com/article.aspx/Cowboys_Tech_led_to_death/L101099085.

-----. "Oklahoma State's New Offensive Coordinator, Mike Yurcich, Is a Virtual Puzzle to Fans." *Tulsa World*. 25 Aug. 2013. http://www.tulsaworld.com/article.aspx/Oklahoma_States_new_offensive_coordinator_is_a_virtual_puzzle_to_fans/20130825_93_B1_CUTLIN976237.

-----. "'One-Heart Team.'" *Tulsa World*. 11 Sept. 2001. http://www.tulsaworld.com/article.axpx/One_heart_team/0109ll_Sp_b1onehe.

-----. "OSU's Golden Thankful." *Tulsa World*. 1 Aug. 1999. http://www.tulsaworld.com/article.aspx/OSUs_Golden_thankful/19990830_Sp_b7osuse.

-----. "OSU's Richetti Jones Can Walk, Talk a Good game." *Tulsa World*. 10 Nov. 2011. http://www.tulsaworld.com/article.axpx./OSUs_Richetti_Jones_can_walk_talk_a_good_game/20111110_93_B1_CUTLIN218782.

-----. "Rader Baffled By Thompson." *Tulsa World*. 16 Sept. 1996. http://www.tulsaworld.com/article.aspx/Rader_Baffled_By_Thompson/19960916_Sp_b1rader.

-----. "Unheralded Recruit Now an Expected Oklahoma State Starter." *Tulsa World*. 20 Aug. 2013. http://www.tulsaworld.com/article/aspx/Unheralded_recuit_now_an_expected_Oklahoma_State_starter/20130820_93_B1_CUTLIN58363.

Tush, Terry. "Artrell Woods Talks About Injury." *GoPokes*. 4 Aug. 2007. http://oklahomastate.scout.com/2/664695.html.

-----. "Bailey's Kick Saves Cowboys." *GoPokes*. 30 Sept. 2010. http://oklahomastate.scout.com/2/1007731.html.

Wahl, Grant. "Portrait of the Artist." *Sports Illustrated*. 13 March 2000. http://sportsillustrated.cnn.com/vault/article/magazine/MAG1018524/index.htm.

# INDEX
## (LAST NAME, DEVOTION DAY NUMBER)

**203**